BUILDING SKILL AND CAPABILITY AMONG GRAM PANCHAYAT PRESIDENTS

By the Same Author

1. Capacity Building for Local Body Leaders
2. Dynamics of New Panchayati Raj System in India (in 15 volumes)
3. Emerging Dimensions in Decentralisation *(In Press)*
4. Ethnic Identity and National Loyalty of Ethnic Group : A case study of Tamil Nadu) *(in Press)*
5. Functional Efficiency of Gram Sabha in Tamil Nadu *(in Press)*
6. Grassroot Democracy in Indian Society
7. New Panchayati Raj System at Work : An Evolution
8. New Panchayati Raj in Tamil Nadu : with Act in Original
9. Process and Performance of Gram Panchayat Women and Dalit Presidents : with 38 case studies of Tamil Nadu Panchayats (*in Press*)
10. Rural Transformation and People's Entitlement's

About the Author

Ganapathy Palanithurai, Professor in Rajiv Gandhi Chair, Gandhigram Rural Institute is an academic activist working with the people in rural areas for building the capacity of the leaders and people to reinvent sustainable grassroots democracy. He is heading the Department of Political Science and Development Administration, in Gandhigram Rural University, Tamil Nadu. His policy advocacy role at the governmental level is increasingly felt at present in all the three levels, namely, sub-regional, regional and national as he does more field work than theorization. He has been associating himself with State Planning Commission of Tamil Nadu, Population Foundation of India, Rajiv Gandhi Foundation, CAPART, Ministry of Rural Areas and Employment and DANIDA (Danish-Indo Development Agency) in specific areas of activities in connection with empowerment of people. He is in the network of the Non-Governmental Organisations for Panchayat activities. He involves himself in capacity building exercise for local body leaders. He has evolved training module and manual for local body leaders. He has to his credit twenty-four books, seventy-five articles in reputed journals, ten working papers, seven monographs, seven review articles on three major areas, namely, Legislative Behaviour, Ethnicity and Panchayati Raj System. He was a recipient of Fellowship from Sastri Indo-Canadian Institute, New Delhi and World Academy of Art and Science, USA. He has visited the US and Canada, on academic assignments. He was a visiting fellow in the MiGill University, Canada in 1989. He is a life member of Indian Institute of Public Administration, Indian Association of Public Administration, Indian Association of Political Science, Indian Association of American Studies, and Indian Association of Canadian Studies. He is a member of the expert committee constituted by the Government of Tamil Nadu, to monitor the training programme for local body leaders.

BUILDING SKILL AND CAPABILITY AMONG GRAM PANCHAYAT PRESIDENTS

An Experience from the Field

G. PALANITHURAI

CONCEPT PUBLISHING COMPANY, NEW DELHI-110059

Cataloging in Publication Data—DK
Courtesy: D.K. Agencies (P) Ltd. <docinfo@dkagencies.com>

Palanithurai, G. (Ganapathy), 1953-
Building skill and capability among gram panchayat presidents : an experience from the field / G. Palanithurai.
p. cm.
Study with reference to Tamil Nadu, India.
Includes bibliographical references (p.)
Includes index.
ISBN 8180691780

1. Panchayat—India—Tamil Nadu. 2. Civic leaders—Training of—India—Tamil Nadu. 3. Decentralization in government—India—Tamil Nadu. I. Title.

DDC 320.840 954 82 21

ISBN 81-8069-178-0

First Published 2005

Published and Printed by
Ashok Kumar Mittal
Concept Publishing Company
A/15-16, Commercial Block, Mohan Garden
NEW DELHI-110059 (India)

Phone : 25351460, 25351794
Fax : 091-11-25357103
E-mail : publishing@conceptpub.com

TO
THE DIVINE MOTHER

Preface

Capacity Building and Training are the two concepts which have been repeatedly discussed in many fora with a view to increase the resourcefulness of the individuals and groups who are involved in specific tasks and discharging assigned responsibilities. In Indian context, business houses are taking up the responsibility of building the capacity and imparting the needed skills to the individuals in order to achieve the target. But at the policy making level, though it was considered as an imperative, there is no initiative to chalk out a comprehensive policy on 'capacity building' for policy makers. As a result our policy making process as well as the process of democracy suffer to a considerable extent.

Recently enunciated "Democratic Decentralization" through the Constitutional Amendments brought to the decision-making system, three million representatives of the people through election and they have to perform a variety of roles. Our policy makers at the central and state level had not visualized the dire need of capacity building for the elected representatives of the grassroots institutions and the officials as they have to face the challenges of decentralization and its implications in the society. As a result without having a sound training policy, training was an *ad hoc* arrangement done sporadically by a few agencies in the absence of training module, training manual and well trained master trainers.

In a total negative climate towards decentralization of powers, the local body leaders had assumed responsibilities and faced plethora of problems to discharge their duties. It is a well known fact that elections were conducted, conformity legislations had been passed in response to the requirements of the Constitution.

Since Gandhigram Rural Institute – Deemed University has got a strong commitment towards empowerment of people and emancipation of women, started its work in the year 1992 immediate to the passing of 73rd Amendment to the Constitution of India. Creating awareness was the first work initiated by the Gandhigram Rural Institute. After the election, capacity building was the main activity undertaken by the institute.

The Gandhigram Rural Institute – Deemed University had created a network of Non-Governmental Development Organisations to undertake this capacity building exercise. Subsequently training module and manual were prepared in consultation with the NGOs, the Panchayat leaders and officials. With the support of the CAPART, Government of India, training programme was conducted. Later refresher programme was conducted periodically for the Panchayat leaders. After the second General Election of Local Bodies, the training module was updated and training programme was conducted for the Gram Panchayat leaders of eight districts. Retired Additional Directors of Rural Development had been taken in as master trainers to conduct the programme. With the support of the CAPART and the Hunger Project entire programme was carried out. Government of Tamil Nadu had passed an order and by which Gandhigram Rural Institute has been recognized as a nodal centre for training. Experience of the training programme in the first period from 1996 to 2001 was recorded and published by the Concept Publishing Company. The second term training experience is totally different from that of the first one. Hence it was decided to brought to popular consumption.

While conducting the training programmes, it has been noticed that many of the Gram Panchayat Leaders had done several innovative activities in Panchayat Administration and Social Development. Equally many of the leaders are in struggle. Even in the training itself, it was decided to bring to light the success and struggles of the Panchayats. As a result a workshop was organised and in which they shared their experiences. This was considered as an impact of the training programme. Hence a report recording the experience of the Panchayat leaders in the workshop has been incorporated in this work.

To complete any task, it requires a team work. To carry out a marathon training programme, a team of trainers helped me. My colleagues equally supported my academic activities. My family members left me to carry out my research activities. Our authorities have extended all possible help to undertake such works since they are relevant to the basic objectives of the institute. Finally, my clients, the Panchayat leaders, who have been involving in all creative activities amplifying my faith that Panchayat institution would deliver goods. For all those who helped me to complete the training work and the documentation work, I express my sincere thanks.

G. Palanithurai

Contents

Preface	*vii*
List of Tables	*xii*
1. Introduction	1
2. Experience of Decentralization in Tamil Nadu	6
3. Training Experience	13
4. Trials and Triumphs of Panchayats	119
5. Observations and Conclusion	154
Appendices	
I. Training Schedule	162
II. Proforma – I	166
III. Proforma – II	167
IV. Proforma – III	168
V. Resource Persons	169
Bibliography	171
Index	173

List of Tables

1.	Distribution of Respondents by Age	50
2.	Distribution of Respondents by Education	51
3.	Distribution of Respondents by Religion	52
4.	Distribution of Respondents by Community	52
5.	Distribution of Respondents by Occupation	53
6.	Distribution of Respondents by Landholdings	54
7.	Distribution of Respondents by Type of Family	54
8.	Distribution of Respondents by Type of Housing	55
9.	Distribution of Respondents by Possessing of Electricity Facility	55
10.	Distribution of Respondents by Possessing of Toilet Facility	56
11.	Distribution of Respondents by Possessing of Water Tap Connection Facility	56
12.	Details of Family Members of the Respondent	57
13.	Party Affiliation of the Respondent	58
14.	Distribution of Respondents by Newspaper Reading Habits	59
15.	Distribution of Respondents by Age group	61
16.	Distribution of Respondents by Educational Qualification	62
17.	Distribution of Respondents by Religion	63
18.	Distribution of Respondents by Community	63
19.	Distribution of Respondents by Occupation	64
20.	Distribution of Respondents by Landholdings	65
21.	Distribution of Respondents by Annual Income	66
22.	Distribution of Respondents by Type of Family	67
23.	Details of House owned by Respondents	67
24.	Type of House	68
25.	Distribution of Household facilities of the Respondents	69
26.	Political Party Affiliation of the Respondents	70
27.	Type of Newspaper Reading	71

1

Introduction

Ten years have gone by and people from all walks of life have started asking what the Panchayats have achieved as it was stated while presenting the Bill in Parliament that Panchayats were created with clear-cut roles to perform as institutions of self-government. There are both positive and negative responses. Extreme romanticization and extreme negation will not serve the purpose. Realistic analysis and evaluation of the process rather than of the end product or outcome of the leaders' or the institutions' performance are necessary. Before undertaking any such analysis and evaluation a realistic consideration of the process of building the institutions and the skills and capabilities of the personnel will help to ensure a proper perspective. While looking at the Panchayats against the backdrop of the enabling conditions, capacity building emerges as the core in the process and thereby it becomes significant. Generally attention is focused on the powers conferred upon the Panchayats. Powers given to the Panchayats have to be digested for which capacity is needed. Without building the capacity devolving power is meaningless. So capacity building assumes prominence. It calls for a few prerequisites that have to be assured. To realize the full implications of decentralization of powers an array of steps have to be taken. They are: needed political will at the State level to push this process of devolution very forcefully as it faces a variety of barriers; a conformity to legislation conforming to the spirit of the 73rd Amendment to the Constitution of India; creating an enabling atmosphere at the State level to devolve powers, functions, functionaries and finance; passing of needed government orders to translate the Act into rules; creating a change in the mindset of the officials favouring devolution of powers; preparing the leaders with needed skills and capacity to manage the Panchayats; and, creating awareness among the people about the new system which has been created through the 73rd Amendment.

To perform the above mentioned tasks, apart from the government a variety of agencies have to be prepared. The roles of intellectuals, the higher level bureaucracy, development institutions, academic institutions, training institutions and the media are significant in the process of devolution. Each one's activity is essential in its own orbit. But capacity building has a special significance as it plays a key role in enabling the Panchayats to perform their roles and functions. Whatever powers have been devolved have to be used and managed properly. Otherwise power on its own will not produce any results. Panchayat management relies wholly on the efficiency of the leaders. So increasing their capabilities and efficiency through capacity building is imperative.

It is unfortunate that the government is not alive to the problem. This issue has been addressed sporadically but systematic efforts are lacking. Except in a few States, capacity building has not drawn the attention of the authorities of the State Government. There is no training policy. Sporadic attempts have been made by a few national and regional institutions but their efforts have not yielded satisfactory results. Training needs are many. First, identification of the training institutions; second, selection of trainers to train the leaders; third, preparing the training module and manual; and, fourth, finalizing the training methodology. The above said tasks have to be finalized before taking up the training programme.

The National Institute of Rural Development has taken some steps. State Institutes of Rural Development have been prepared for this task. Regional Extension Training Centres have been selected for training the Panchayat leaders. Unfortunately these institutions are not in a position to provide effective training since they are perceived as condemned institutions because unwanted officials have been dumped in all these training institutions. Hence everyone wonders whether effective training can be given by these institutions. Assuming that they can, to what extent can they cover the entire leaders of the Panchayati

Raj System? Moreover the devolution process is in many different stages in many States. It is not uniform in all the States. In one State elections have not been conducted, while in another State elections have been conducted but responsibilities have not been devolved; and, in yet another State responsibilities have been devolved but finance has not been distributed.

Against this background, it is necessary to trace the training experience in India. Non-Governmental development organizations have conducted training programmes for Panchayat leaders, that too at the lowest level. Government institutions have conducted training programmes for Panchayat leaders, not as professional trainers, but just to justify their existence by conducting the earmarked training programmes.

The whole gamut of training Panchayati Raj leaders has been studied deeply by Prof. M. Aslam with the support of the Ford Foundation. He has identified the training facilities, the capacity of the training teams and the training methodology. He has found a number of weaknesses in the training programmes conducted by the training institutions, primarily the training institutions' lack of training strategy, poor needs assessment, lack of coordinated approach, and lack of direction. As a result of these one finds confusion among both leaders and functionaries about the concept and profile of the Panchayat Raj System. To set right this confusion steps have been taken by various development institutions throughout the country with a clear-cut strategy. In this context the Rajiv Gandhi Chair for Panchayati Raj Studies has taken up the responsibility of training the leaders at the grassroots.

There are many steps in conducting an effective training programme. First, a training manual has to be prepared. Secondly, a training module has to be evolved. Thirdly, a committed team of master trainers has to be developed. Information to be provided to the Panchayat leaders, namely Panchayat Act, Panchayat rules, Government orders, Government schemes for rural development and financial institutions providing financial support for rural development activities have to be listed and collected. Training materials to be used in the training programme have to be procured. A training methodology has to be evolved. Training venue and training atmosphere are the most important prerequisites for adducing importance to the training. While evolving the training methodology it has to be borne in mind that the leaders who are going to be trained in the programme have varied educational background from illiteracy to post-graduation. To facilitate easy learning the training should be provided in the discussion and dialogue mode. The teaching mode has to be totally avoided. Officials who are in service should not be allowed to take classes as they can force the trainees to listen to them and even intimidate them. Officials may join the training programme and if the trainer commits any mistake regarding the rules it can be pointed out. Beyond this the officials should have no role in the training programme.

Bringing leaders to the training venue is very important. It is necessary that the training institutions should have close contact with the government in this regard. A specific government order is necessary to mobilize the leaders for the training.

The Rajiv Gandhi Chair for Panchayati Raj Studies prepared a training module and a manual and the same has been published. The Rajiv Gandhi Foundation and the Ford Foundation helped the Chair to prepare the manual. It is an elaborate and comprehensive manual prepared with the help of experts and based on the needs assessment and the experience of the Chair in conducting training programmes in the past five years. It was tested and a pilot run was conducted. The manual was published only after making corrections based on the suggestions that emerged. It took nearly one year. There is yet another module which has been prepared for women. It is a leadership training module. It has been prepared by a team of experts specializing in empowering women. It is meant for the whole of India. For the Tamil Nadu context, the Rajiv Gandhi Chair has translated the material into the vernacular (Tamil) with slight modifications to suit local requirements. This has been published for circulation and distribution among the training institutions.

Further, after testing the module, an information package consisting of the updated Tamil Nadu Panchayat Act, rules, government orders, recommendations of the First and the Second Finance Commissions and programmes and schemes of Central and State governments has been prepared and this has also been published for distribution among the leaders of Local Bodies.

A well-trained and committed team is essential for conducting a training programme. The Chair has identified five resource persons at the level of Additional Director of Rural Development. They are all retired officials. They are all pro-Panchayat. They have established their grip over the subject. Along with them the Rajiv Gandhi Chair team of trainers have also been trained thoroughly.

Residential places have been identified as the best locations for training programmes. Since all the programmes are residential it is necessary that the atmosphere in the training institution should be learner friendly.

To mobilize the leaders from their respective places to the training spot steps have been taken at the Government level by asking the Government to issue an order. Accordingly the Government of Tamil Nadu issued an order, No.28/RD/C3 dated 1-4-2003, which pronounces that the training programme conducted by Gandhigram Rural Institute under the aegis of the Rajiv Gandhi Chair for Panchayati Raj Studies is officially recognized and the district administrations have been asked to take steps to mobilize the Panchayati leaders for the training.

After all these steps were taken the training programme was conducted.

The entire training experience has been explained in two chapters as there were two specific programmes. One was the training programme conducted for male Gram Panchayati Presidents while the other was conducted for women. The last chapter furnishes the observations and conclusions.

2

Experience of Decentralization in Tamil Nadu

It is curious that the experience of democratic decentralization of power varies from country to country and, in India, from province to province. It varies extensively even among districts. Varieties of perspectives have been developed on the concept and practice of democratic decentralization. Democratic decentralization of powers empowers the majority of the people, who have hitherto been powerless and voiceless, by disempowering a few sections who continue to hold power. It is a difficult task and a painful process. Further this process needs a very strong commitment and energy on the part of the leader who spearheads the devolution of powers to curtail the implications of the activities of the powerful sections who have hitherto enjoyed power and benefits. Yet another important aspect in the process is that the new stakeholders in governance have to be alerted and activated to participate in the process, for which a grassroots movement has to be built up from the bottom. As and when power devolves, the stakeholders who are on the lines should have the power to absorb the devolved powers. It is a well known fact that India is a land of paradoxes and riddles. The latest paradox is that decentralized governance is perceived differently by different players and stakeholders in the process of decentralization of powers.

In India it is a centralized move, and not based on the demand from below, to decentralize powers to the grassroots. There is absolutely no movement of the people to takeover power. People have demands and the Government has no mechanism to meet the demands of the people. There is a gap between the people and the Government. There are conscious efforts on the part of the Government to bridge the gap between the people and the Government. Decentralization of powers has several objectives of which the principal one is bringing people closer to the Government and making people participate in governance. These activities are taking place in different names in different regions. Decentralization is popular and holds many promises. They are: protecting the self-respect of the people, bringing people closer to the Government, transforming the beneficiaries into citizens, changing activities from a supply driven mode to a demand driven one, making the people participate in the process of development, strengthening democracy, looking at issues from the perspective of the people, delegating responsibilities to the people, reducing the cost of governance, making the administration transparent, enhancing the responsiveness of the Government to the people, enlarging opportunities to citizens to participate in decision making, drawing on and using local knowledge for development, achieving economic development, evolving informal local mechanisms for the management of resources, achieving social justice, promoting partnership between state and society, planning from below, developing a greater sense of ownership of development projects, enhancing the capacity of the people, enlarging associational activities at a lower level, facilitating cooperation between government, local level organizations and NGOs, enhancing the accountability of bureaucrats and representatives, easing the frustrations of the people by enabling them to play official roles, building the skills of the people, improving the collective action potential of rural inhabitants, facilitating monitoring and evaluating of plans from below, undermining the authoritarian enclaves, promoting a more equitable distribution of resources, building civic culture, empowering women, enhancing the legitimacy of the political system, and, nurturing a pro-poor, pro-women and pro-nature atmosphere.

These promises can be fulfilled only by concerted action for altering the structure of the institutions involved in development activities. Initiatives are to be taken from the Central Government to the State Governments and from the State Governments to the Local Bodies. Unless these initiatives are taken, the implications of decentralization cannot be seen on the ground. The 73rd Amendment to the Constitution of India is the first step taken at the federal level. The exercise does not stop with the amendment. Major measures enabling the Panchayats to act as institutions of self-government have to be taken by the State Governments, starting with the enacting of a conformity legislation in the State. After passing the conformity legislation, the State Government has to prepare rules for the operationalization of the Act. It has to prepare the leaders of the grassroots institutions to perform their assigned roles and fulfil their responsibilities by building up the capacity of the leaders. Panchayat functionaries have to be sensitized to the reality of decentralized governance with the participation of the people. The mindset of the bureaucracy has to be changed. To create a conducive environment for the effective functioning of the grassroots institutions the people have to be conscientised. Unless all these steps are taken properly decentralization will not work effectively. Against this background the process of democratic decentralization of powers in Tamil Nadu is being analyzed in this work.

For the past three decades Tamil Nadu politics and government have been under the control of the two ethnic political parties, the DMK and the AIADMK, which are supposed to have worked for the devolution of powers for speedy social transformation. But they are opposed to devolution of powers from the State to the grassroots institutions and support only the devolution of powers from the Centre to the State. Tamil Nadu is known for having postponed the local body elections sixteen times by giving seventeen reasons and for defeating the 64th Constitutional Amendment Bill. The two political parties never concur on any single issue but both concurred in opposing the proposal for creating the three-tier Panchayat system constitutionally. The representatives of these two political parties raised their voice against the three-tier system in Parliament. After the passing of the 73rd Constitutional Amendment Act, Tamil Nadu took one year to bring out a conformity legislation in the year 1994 with several inconsistencies and inbuilt weaknesses contradicting the spirit of the Constitutional Amendment Act. Yet elections were not conducted. In the year 1996 elections were conducted to local bodies and steps were taken to devolve powers to the three tiers of the Panchayati Raj System. The L.C. Jain Committee made clear-cut recommendations for devolution of powers. But these recommendations have not been fully implemented. By conferring only recommendatory and supervisory powers and dividing the schemes for implementation among the three tiers of the Panchayati Raj System, the Panchayats have been made agents of the State Government to carry out their works. So far more than forty-five changes have been effected through amendments in the Panchayat Act. For Gram Panchayats alone 84 Government Orders have been passed. But none of them has reached the Panchayat leaders. As per the 73rd Amendment, powers have to be conferred upon Panchayats through law. But it is unfortunate that all the powers have been conferred upon Panchayats through GOs. The officials who have to help the Panchayat leaders in Panchayat administration are not clear about their roles and responsibilities and, as a result, they have started controlling the Panchayats without looking into the provisions of the Act. Their mindset has not changed. Likewise local body leaders who do not know their roles and responsibilities and the powers conferred upon Panchayats manage the Panchayats as per the guidance of Panchayat clerks who are also novices in administration. Their capacity has to be enhanced to the level of the workload of the Panchayats. The above mentioned factors work as obstacles to establishing the Panchayat institutions as institutions of self-government.

Any role can be performed perfectly by individuals or groups only if they have a clear-cut role perception. The New Panchayati Raj System seeks to establish the Panchayat on a sustainable basis as an institution of self-government. This institutional mechanism has got tremendous potential to deliver services to the people but it is not being perceived as an institution of self-government either by the leaders of local bodies or the bureaucrats. The leaders cannot perceive it properly as an institution of self-government due to lack of orientation and training but the officials, that too at the lower level, deliberately try to subvert the whole process and covertly and overtly turn the Panchayat leaders into contractors by giving work to them from the Central and State Government schemes.

After carrying out the work, while submitting accounts and bills, they submit their leadership also and bend themselves before the Block Development officials to get clearance whereupon the officials establish their supremacy.

The officials who scrutinize the bills raise objections and queries for which the Panchayat Presidents have to respond in the way they expect. Otherwise the leaders will be informed through the Panchayat clerk that provision 205 of the Tamil Nadu Panchayat Act will be invoked under the pretext that the Panchayat President has misappropriated funds. Panchayat Presidents are not accountants to keep accounts and even the Panchayat clerks who are also novices in administration cannot keep accounts as in any Government office because both the Panchayat Presidents and the Panchayat clerks have not been trained in accounting and auditing. To circumvent this problem the Panchayat Presidents have to mend and bend themselves and toe the line of the officials and coopt themselves in the corrupt practices which the officials have developed over a period of time. There are Panchayat Presidents who are clear in their perception of the local bodies and assert themselves as leaders and argue with officials on an equal footing to assert their status. But the officials somehow or the other develop devices to bring them to heel and try to convince the leaders to get into their own corrupt track and trap. Though the number is small, there are leaders with a sense of commitment pursuing their course but they have to struggle hard.

To overcome this problem, everyone suggests that the Panchayat leaders are to be trained properly and their managerial skill to be enhanced. Training the local body leaders is not an easy task as the administrative procedures are highly complicated and the information to be provided to Panchayat leaders is voluminous. Only those well-versed in Panchayat administration can provide training. But it is government officials who give training to Panchayat leaders. They start with what not to do and the attendant implications and stretch it to the suspension and removal of Panchayat Presidents by invoking provision 205 of the Tamil Nadu Panchayat Act. One of the officials who attended a training programme along with Panchayat leaders in Gandhigram Rural Institute complained to the Coordinator that the way

Gandhigram Rural Institute gives training in all the districts officials like him would become powerless and incapable of controlling the Panchayat leaders and that the Panchayat leaders will act independently. Who will control the Panchayat leaders is another basic question of the officials. The officials, from the Assistant Director of Panchayats to the clerk working in the Panchayat office, want the Panchayat leaders to work under their supervision and control as if they only know the procedures and they are the only honest persons in the orbit of governance.

The officials who attended the training programme told the resource persons that they should not be asked questions in the training programme because till date the Panchayat Presidents believe that the officials are well-versed in the rules and procedures of Panchayat administration. By their dominant attitude the officials have established their supremacy over the leaders and the leaders look to the officials, however low their level is, as deciding authorities because of ignorance. It is the experience of the leaders that only very few officials at the lower level are honest and decent in their behaviour and dealings. Officials are also handicapped as they do not know the full implications of the democratic decentralization of powers. Further they cannot identify the weaknesses in the system. Both leaders and officials do not have any administrative manual for day-to-day reference regarding administration.

Activities in the rural areas are being carried out by a number of sectoral departments apart from the rural development departments. As per the powers conferred upon the Panchayats, the sectoral departments have to carry out schemes and programmes with the cooperation and supervision of the Panchayats. The Panchayats have to help the sectoral departments to implement the schemes and they have to identify the beneficiaries through the Gram Sabha. But the officials of the sectoral departments never consult the Panchayats. They do not even inform the Panchayats about what they do in the Panchayat areas. While selecting beneficiaries they do not even consult the Panchayats.

Likewise, the MLAs and the MPs, in utilizing their grants, can consult the Panchayats. But, quite unfortunately, on many occasions, they carry out works independently and, as a result, the demands discussed in the Gram Sabha are unmet though huge amounts of money are spent in the rural areas on various activities. Both MLAs and MPs see to it that the local body leaders do not emerge as local leaders since, in that case, their own supremacy will be challenged. It is also true that, wherever the Panchayat leaders are capable, they are able to bargain with the MLAs and the MPs.

To change the existing scenario, a dynamic drive has to be initiated both from above and below. Both officials and leaders have to be trained and provided with needed information. To fulfil the above task the Rajiv Gandhi Chair for Panchayati Raj Studies of Gandhigram Rural Institute took the initiative. With the support of the Government of India and the Hunger Project, nearly 2500 Gram Panchayat leaders have been trained with the help of dedicated and committed resource persons at as high a level as a retired Additional Director of Rural Development. The amended Panchayat Act, along with Rules and Government Schemes, have been given to the Panchayat leaders. By sensitizing the media through a series of workshops on decentralization, media representatives have been oriented to look at issues at the grassroots from a new perspective. A series of research studies have been carried out on the issues of local governance for policy advocacy. A training manual has been prepared for conducting training for Panchayat leaders and copies have been distributed to NGOs who are involved in Panchayati Raj activities. Yet another training module has been prepared and published for the purpose of conducting leadership training programme for elected women representatives. A textbook has been prepared for students to pursue a course in local governance in Social Sciences degree programmes of the universities of Tamil Nadu. A local body leaders' federation has been formed to voice their issues on their own. A network among the NGOs has been created to synergise their activities to make local governance good governance. To fulfil the constitutional obligation, steps were taken by the State authorities but the spirit of decentralization was lost. In this scenario, in order to realize the true spirit of decentralization, a band of honest and committed leaders in local bodies are working tirelessly and innovatively with the cooperation of good officials and NGOs and they are engaged in a struggle to change the system.

3

Training Experience

Introduction

To increase the efficiency of an individual in performing assigned roles and responsibilities continuous capacity building is imperative. The success of the first Government, Local Self-Government, depends on a number of factors in which capacity building plays an important role. In Tamil Nadu the Gram Panchayat Presidents have to perform twin roles, namely that of the elected Panchayat leader and that of the executive authority. Unless their managerial skill is improved there can be no effective delivery of services to the people in the Panchayats. It has been the lament of the leaders that they are not properly oriented in Panchayat administration and they are not provided with needed information. To overcome this obstacle the Rajiv Gandhi Chair has conducted capacity building exercises for Gram Panchayati leaders of eight districts, namely, Pudukkottai, Tiruchirappalli, Dindigul, Sivagangai, Ramanathapuram, Virudhunagar, Theni and Karur with the support of CAPART, Hyderabad.

Collaboration with District Administration

Before the commencement of this exercise in the eight districts, an order was issued by the Director of Rural Development of Government of Tamil Nadu by which the District administrations were asked to make use of this opportunity and conduct the capacity building exercise for Gram Panchayat leaders. The District Panchayat Secretary was made the nodal officer for training to help the Rajiv Gandhi Chair. Accordingly, the District Collectors were approached by the Coordinator of the Rajiv Gandhi Chair to help the team ensure attendance in the training programme. Highly enthusiastic, energetic and committed District Collectors took steps through their officials to mobilize the leaders to attend the training programme. They insisted that, in the training programme, social development issues had to be discussed and the Panchayat leaders were to be sensitized on social development issues.

Orders were passed and instructions were given to the Assistant Director for Panchayats and Block Development Officers that they had to send the Panchayati leaders for training. For each Block, one Deputy Block Development Officer was assigned the duty of ensuring attendance in the training programme on all the three days. Everyday the earmarked officer took attendance and reported to the Assistant Director of Panchayats about the progress of the training programme through phone.

Inauguration

The first batch of the training programme was inaugurated by Shri S. Ayyar, I.A.S., Director of Rural Development, Government of Tamil Nadu. While inaugurating the training programme, he explicitly indicated the need for capacity building as Panchayat activities have increased enormously. Further he reiterated that Panchayat leaders, by equipping themselves, have to prepare and declare themselves as master trainers to train grassroots level leaders. He also stressed that Panchayat leaders have to concentrate on social development issues which are so vital for achieving sustainable rural development. The trainees were asked to express their problems in Panchayat administration. For each and every question he patiently gave answers. The interactive session was quite impressive. Finally, he reiterated the fact that this space has to be considered as space for development and not for politics. He pleaded that Panchayat leaders should show the way to others in bringing about excellence in performance. The Director of Rural Development finally said that frequent interaction between the higher level officials and the Panchayat Presidents would solve many of the problems in Panchayat administration. In each district the training programme was inaugurated either by the District Collector or by the Project Officer, DRDA as it would give a more official tone to the training programme which was conducted in training institutions and not in any government office.

Introductory Remarks

Dr. G. Palanithurai, while briefing the participants about the training, made a few observations.

Generally the elected representatives from local bodies have the mindset that training is not needed. One should study Indian democracy and the mindset of the politicians. Once an individual is elected either to Parliament or to Legislature, he or she feels that he/she knows everything. Moreover there is no training for them. This is the prevailing level of Indian democracy. The elected representatives are not serious about equipping themselves as efficient legislators or parliamentarians. Though these poorly oriented elected representatives have the power and responsibility to decide the policies and programmes for the growth and development of the people of India.

We can draw lessons from the most popular democratic country, namely the USA. One can observe that in the USA among the elected representatives, there are several professionals like academicians, medical practitioners, engineers, business magnates, journalists and so on. It means that they come from a knowledge society. Yet all of them have to undergo a period of one month's training in the Kennedy School of Government. After this orientation only they take part in the deliberations of the Congress.

The Indian context is unique and different. Within a day the elected representatives feel that they have undergone a transformation. They change their dress, shoes or sandals etc., but they do not give much attention to orienting and equipping themselves in terms of skill and capacity to perform effectively their roles and responsibilities.

As the Panchayat Raj System of governance is a new one and has to work with the people directly, the elected representatives of local bodies particularly the Presidents of Gram Panchayats need proper orientation and training. India does not progress because our representatives exhibit poor leadership. Other countries like Japan, South Korea, Singapore, Taiwan have attained progress within two to three decades after they attained independence because of their leadership. Still 35 per cent of the Indian population is below the poverty line. Managerial skills needed to effectively manage the affairs of a family, state and nation are the need of the hour.

Among the various elected representatives training is very much needed to the Gram Panchayat Presidents as the Gram Panchayat is the basic unit of Panchayat administration. They have to perform the duties of an executive authority as well as those of the President of the Panchayat. Villagers can easily approach the Gram Panchayat Presidents while a member of the Legislative Assembly or Parliament is not easily accessible to them. After the establishment of the New Panchayat Raj System the expectation and perception of the common people have changed. If the elected representatives of these bodies fail to perform effectively there is definitely a setback to the village and the nation.

Leaders do not know the concepts of decentralization, people's participation, resource mobilization, micro planning, social development and the administrative system, procedures, rules and regulations of governance. They are not able to visualize the scope and implications of Gram Panchayat.

Leadership is a learning process. A learner should first understand the changing environment in which she or he has to work or function and accordingly change her or his mindset. In the context of the change she or he should effect necessary modifications in personal habits and equip himself or herself to function effectively. Leaders of all levels have to undergo this process. Programmed training will speed up the process. A trainee should have faith in training and she or he must sincerely orient himself/herself during the training.

The elected representatives of local bodies entered the PRIs as brave leaders. In course of time they become contractors. Most of them spend their tenure as good contractors providing basic amenities in their villages. But the expected economic development and social justice have not been attained in their villages. Before they can understand the concept and system of Panchayati Raj, the tenure comes to an end.

There are successful elected representatives in Tamil Nadu who, in spite of the constraints and handicaps in PRIs, perform their roles effectively. They swim against the current after they orient themselves through training. Success is nothing but the power of mind. Dr. G. Palanithurai appealed to the participants to make use of the training opportunity to strengthen their mind and enhance their skills for administering the Gram Panchayat.

Sessions Input

Dr. G. Palanithurai explained the promises of decentralization of powers. The promises are the basic objectives of decentralization of powers.

After more than sixty years of experience in centralization of powers and resources 80 per cent of developing and transitional countries of Eastern and Central Europe and the former Soviet Union, along with Afro-Asian countries, have started the new experiment of democratic decentralization of powers as centralization of powers and resources did not achieve development and reduce poverty through the top-down approach to development. More precisely, after the mid-1980s 'decentralization' is a concept practiced vigorously in 63 countries in the world in the context of Globalization. It is being practised with the following objectives :

- (i) Protecting the self-respect of the people,
- (ii) Bringing people closer to the Government,
- (iii) Changing the mind set from beneficiaries to citizens,
- (iv) Narrowing the gap between the people and the government,
- (v) Shifting from supply driven to demand driven mode,
- (vi) Making the people participate in the process of development,
- (vii) Deepening democracy,
- (viii) Looking at issues from the perspective of the people,
- (ix) Giving responsibilities to the people,
- (x) Reducing the cost of governance,
- (xi) Making the administration transparent,
- (xii) Enhancing the responsiveness of the government to the people,
- (xiii) Enlarging opportunities to citizens to participate in decision making,
- (xiv) Drawing and using local knowledge for development,

(xv) Achieving economic development,
(xvi) Designing informal local mechanisms for the management of resources,
(xvii) Achieving social justice,
(xviii) Promoting partnership between state and society,
(xix) Ensuring planning from below,
(xx) Developing greater sense of ownership of development projects,
(xxi) Enhancing the capacity of the people,
(xxii) Enhancing associational activities at a lower level,
(xxiii) Facilitating cooperation between government, local level organizations and NGOs,
(xxiv) Enhancing the accountability of bureaucrats and representatives,
(xxv) Easing the frustrations of the people by enabling them to play official roles,
(xxvi) Building the skills of the people,
(xxvii) Improving the collective action potential of rural dwellers,
(xxviii) Promoting planning, monitoring and evaluating from below,
(xxix) Undermining the authoritarian enclaves,
(xxx) Promoting a more equitable distribution of resources,
(xxxi) Building civic culture,
(xxxii) Empowering women,
(xxxiii) Enhancing the legitimacy of the political system,
(xxxiv) Functioning pro-poor,
(xxxv) Functioning pro-women, and
(xxxvi) Functioning pro-nature.

But the results are yet to come from the world to confirm whether the objectives of decentralization have been realized. Reports of cursory analysis reveal positive trends. Yet, to make concrete observations, one has to wait for authentic and comprehensive results.

In the Indian context the 73rd Amendment to the Constitution of India is a framework to devolve or democratically decentralize powers from the federal government to the people. It is only a guiding principle through which power has to be devolved.

To evaluate the decentralization process in India one has to keep in mind the backdrop of the framework evolved by the federal government under the leadership of late Prime Minister Rajiv Gandhi. He made a presentation in the Parliament when he introduced the 64th Amendment Bill to the Constitution of India and this has been termed a framework of decentralization of powers in India. It has two major mandates, namely effecting changes in the process of governance and in development. It unequivocally states that the existing "we govern you participate" syndrome has to be changed to "you govern yourself and you participate". Likewise the present scenario of supply driven bureaucratic development initiatives has to be replaced by demand driven participatory development. Therefore, the new initiatives in India for democratic decentralization have to focus on :

(i) Economic development,
(ii) Social justice,
(iii) People's initiatives,
(iv) Harnessing local knowledge for the market,
(v) Upgrading of local skills for productive activities,
(vi) Synergyzing the evolved people's institutions and newly created institutions through the Constitution,
(vii) Adopting local models of management to manage local resources for optimal and effective use,
(viii) Democratizing people's institutions, and
(ix) People's programmes and government's participation.

The whole process of decentralization of powers has to be carried out in such a way that the institutions that are created through law have to integrate themselves with the institutions evolved by the people over a period of time. The imposed institutions should have resilience to absorb the evolved institutions in delivering services to the people. By doing this, the institutions will acquire the character of participation. The stakeholders will takeover the ownership of the institution only when the institutions respond to the demands of the people. One cannot expect that the devolution will take place uniformly throughout the country and the states. It will vary from region to region and even district to district. Likewise delivery of services will also vary from region to region and from district to district.

The decentralization process requires a lot of exercises, understanding of the rural realities, capacity of the local level leaders apart from the political will of the state level leaders and legal requirements. In India experience shows a variety of models of decentralization emerging as the ground level is not uniform throughout. More specifically Tamil Nadu presents its own distinct characteristics of devolution. The existing devolution does not anchor on people but is more centred round the Panchayat leader. Ambiguous perception on the part of the representatives of the people, the bureaucrats and the people themselves of decentralization deters the process of devolution of powers and its implications. Along with the Panchayat there are many institutions and organizations performing certain assigned and assumed roles and responsibilities to achieve development in the society. To work with people's institutions and organizations, the Panchayats have to develop a new framework in which the stakeholders should have responsibilities so that the Panchayats move towards the people rather than the government. People and their institutions matter much in the process of governance and development.

After elaborately explaining the basic objectives, Palanithurai narrated the steps taken by the Government of India to incorporate them in the Constitution of India. He explained the following basic features of the 73rd Amendment to the Constitution of India :

(a) Constitutional entity,
(b) New dimension in federalism,
(c) Establishing direct democracy – Gram Sabha,
(d) Planning from below,
(e) Three-tier structure,
(f) One-third seats are reserved for women,
(g) Seats are reserved for *Dalits* proportionate to their population,
(h) Establishing State Finance Commission,
(i) Establishing State Election Commission,
(j) District Planning Committee, and
(k) 29 subjects in 11th Schedule.

Panchayat Administration (Core Faculty)

1. Introduction about the Panchayat and its administrative aspects.
2. Important provisions of the TN Panchayats Act, 1994 with reference to Panchayat administration.
3. Status of the Gram Panchayats prior to 1994 and after 1994, (i.e.) after the commencement of the new Act.
4. Mandatory functions of Gram Panchayat are :

   (i) Providing water for drinking, washing and bathing purposes.
   (ii) Formation and maintenance of roads.
   (iii) Provision of streetlights and their maintenance.
   (iv) Construction and maintenance of side drains and storm water drains.
   (v) Sanitary work including cleaning of streets, removal of debris and unwanted rubbish and filth.
   (vi) Provision of public latrines and their maintenance.
   (vii) Provision and maintenance of burning and burial grounds.
   (viii) Such other duty as may be assigned to the Gram Panchayats by Government from time to time.

5. Discretionary functions of Gram Panchayat :

   (a) Planting of trees on roadsides.
   (b) Provisions of light on public roads.
   (c) Provision of market procedure and income generation aspects.
   (d) Fairs and festivals – providing sanitary arrangement for village festivals.
   (e) Providing cart stand, cattle shed.
   (f) Public landing places – bus stop, bus shelter.
   (g) Providing public slaughter houses and issue of licences to slaughter houses.
   (h) Providing reading rooms in villages.
   (i) Opening of literacy centres and social education centres.

(j) Construction of building for television sets and radios.
(k) Provision of playground and park.
(l) Construction of building and making necessary provision for improving the health, culture, comfort and entertainment and common facilities for the residents of the Gram Panchayat – how to plan and execute.

6. Agency functions of Gram Panchayat.
7. Role of the Gram Panchayat in the process of planning for economic development and social justice – brief outline of planning.
8. Powers of the Gram Panchayat enabling it to achieve its goal – what are they?
9. Functions of the President and his/her powers.
10. Functions of the executive authority and his/her responsibilities.

Functions of Executive Authority

The President is nominated as the executive authority by notification under the T.N. Panchayats Act. His functions include :

(a) Initiating action on all resolutions.
(b) Assessment of tax under all items.
(c) Collection of taxes – coercive steps to be taken including distraint proceedings.
(d) Conduct of auction and leasing out of properties and rights of Gram Panchayat.
(e) Preparation of agenda and its timely service to members.
(f) Controlling employees and extracting work from them.
(g) Appointment of officers and staff by following the procedures.
(h) Preparation of budget, annual accounts, and administration report.
(i) Preparation of development plan.
(j) Emergency powers of the executive authority.
(k) Role of Gram Panchayat in providing basic amenities to its residents.

(l) Maintenance of drinking water sources, roads, street lights and sanitation.

(m) Points highlighted in day to day administration of Gram Panchayats.

(n) Execution of minor works upto Rs.2,000 without measurement and check measurement.

(o) Repair of hand pump and power pump – procedure and ceiling amount.

(p) Norms for replacing bills and other accessories in streetlight maintenance.

(q) Utilizing the service of charted engineer for estimate costing up to a lakh of rupees.

(r) Building plan approval.

(s) Issue of licence and granting permission for installation of machines.

(t) Providing house connection for drinking water – procedure to be followed.

Panchayat Finance

Sources of Income of Gram Panchayats :

A. Tax and Sources

1. House Tax
2. Professional Tax
3. Advertisement Tax
4. Tax on Agricultural Lands
5. Library Tax

B. Assigned Revenues

B1. Statutory Revenues

1. Local Cess
2. Surcharge on Stamp Duty

B2. Statutory Grants – Receipts

1. Entertainment Tax
2. State Finance Commission Grants
3. Central Finance Commission Grants
4. Surcharge Tax from Quarries.

C. Non-Statutory Grants

1. Cremation Grant
2. Share of Quarry Auction Amount

D. Other Non-Tax Sources

1. Levy of licence fees for various purposes

   (a) Levy of licence fees for dangerous and offensive trades.
   (b) Collection of fees from private cart stands.
   (c) Collection of fees from private markets.
   (d) Licensing of dogs and pigs.
   (e) Licensing of erection of pandal temporarily and collection of licence fees for similar items for trade, use of Panchayat properties and enjoyment of usufructs of trees etc.

Taxes

House Tax

1. Basis of levy of house tax :

   (a) Capital value,
   (b) Annual public value,
   (c) On plinth area basis.

2. Rates of house tax on various bases.
3. Buildings exempted from house tax.
4. State Government buildings are liable to pay house tax.
5. Levy or surcharge on house tax :

(a) For small business buildings – 20 per cent on house tax.
(b) For big business buildings – 60 per ecnt on house tax.

6. Procedure for collection of house tax.
7. Action to be taken upon non-payment of tax :

   (a) Details of distraint proceedings.
   (b) Prosecution to be launched for collection of taxes and fees.

8. Write off of irrecoverable taxes.

Profession Tax

Basis of Levy

1. Collection of profession tax from employees.
2. Collection of profession tax from persons doing business.
3. Obligation on the part of employer and businessmen to furnish half yearly statement of salary paid to employees and of half yearly business turnover to the Gram Panchayat.
4. Employees and businessmen have to deduct profession tax from the salaries of employees and pay it to the Panchayat.
5. Rates of Profession Tax.
6. Action to be taken if employees and businessmen fail to furnish statement and pay tax.

Advertisement Tax

1. Advertisements exempted from tax.
2. Basis of levy of advertisement tax :

   (a) Erection of boards and hoardings.
   (b) Advertisement through wall painting.

3. Rates of advertisement tax.

4. Advertisement tax to be collected annually.
5. Procedure to be followed when one fails to pay tax.

Tax on Agricultural Land

1. Difference of this tax from the routine land revenue.
2. Reasons for which agricultural land tax can be levied.
3. Rates of tax and productivity of levy is based on the requirement of the project cost or contribution amount to be remitted for development schemes.
4. Levy of tax in special meeting convened by the Panchayat.
5. District Collector's sanction required.
6. Demand to be settled by the Village Administrative Officer and if the Panchayat so desires the collection work can be entrusted to him.

Approval of Layouts

A. Layout

1. What is a layout?
2. Application to be collected in prescribed Form 'A'.
3. Owner of land only to apply.
4. Conditions for approval of layout.
5. Land for streets, pathways etc., indicated in layout to be handed over to Gram Panchayat.
6. Estimated cost of laying of streets and pathways to be paid in advance to Panchayat.
7. State Highways Department permission to be obtained if the layout is proposed near Highway road.
8. To be away from railway line, burning ghats and burial grounds.
9. Panchayat to send layout applications to the Deputy Director, Town and Country Planning, located at district headquarters.
10. 10 per cent of layout land to be set apart for common purposes.
11. Application for construction of buildings in Form 'B'.

12. Power of Panchayat to remove construction without permission and approval by Panchayat.
13. Fees to be collected for layout and building construction.

Accounting Procedure

1. Various accounts to be maintained by the Gram Panchayat and their maintenance.
2. Maintenance of various registers and forms prescribed by the Government.
3. Crediting of received taxes and other sources of income – modes and procedures.
4. Expenditure – norms to be followed.
5. Monthly reconciliation of accounts by the Gram Panchayat President and its importance.
6. No direct expenditure can be made from receipts.
7. Checking of receipt books, collection register, *chitta* and cash book.
8. Cheque book to be in the custody of Gram Panchayat President only.
9. Collection of receipt-books – only one book to be sealed with facsimile of President's signature and second book to be issued after receiving completed first collection book.

Meeting Procedure

– Panchayat as a corporate body (Sec. 6).
– It can transact business only by passing resolutions in its meeting.
– President has to convene the meeting (Sec. 46).
– For a meeting to be valid:

  (i) It should be properly convened.
  (ii) It should be properly constituted.
  (iii) It should be held in accordance with the rules.

– Meeting has to be held in the Panchayat office.
– No meeting on holidays.
– Proper notice should be given for the meeting.
– Meeting at least once in a month.
– Agenda should be given to all the members.

Kinds of Meetings

1. Ordinary Meeting – Notice of 3 full days should be given.
2. Urgent meeting – Notice of even less than 24 hours sufficient.
3. Special meeting – Only one subject should be discussed.
4. Requisition meeting– Convened at the request of the members.

- Agenda to be prepared by the President.
- Mode of serving notice:

  (i) By personal service,
  (ii) By serving to any adult member in the family,
  (iii) By RPAD, or
  (iv) By affixing in the last known place of residence of member.

- If proper notice is not given the whole meeting will be invalid.
- Quorum for the meeting is 1/3rd of the members or 3 whichever is higher.
- Resolutions will be decided by majority or consensus.
- In case of deadlock the President will have a second vote or casting vote.
- President will have full powers to regulate proceedings of the meeting.
- Members can also move resolutions after giving proper notice.
- Signature should be obtained in the attendance register and in the minutes book.
- President should preside over the meeting.
- Not more than 60 days should lapse between two meetings.

Common Properties of Panchayat

- Panchayat owns both movable and immovable properties.

- Property can also be acquired.
- Panchayat has a duty to maintain the properties.
- Besides the movable and immovable properties the following *poramboke* lands vest with the Panchayat :

    (a) Unreserved forests.
    (b) Public pathways.
    (c) Tanks, *ooranis*, springs etc.
    (d) Grazing ground.
    (e) Burial ground and burning *ghat*.
    (f) *Manthai poramboke*.
    (g) Threshing ground.
    (h) *Tope poramboke*.
    (i) Cart stands.

Panchayats can use the *poramboke* for the purpose for which it is intended or lease it out for one year.

- If it is to be leased out for more than a year the sanction of the District Collector has to be obtained.
- If the land is to be used for a purpose other than that for which it is intended the District Collector's sanction has to be obtained.
- Panchayat can utilize the *poramboke* lands in ex-*zamin* villages.
- Panchayat can utilize the following *porambokes,* if they are vacant:

    (a) *Natham*,
    (b) Assessed waste,
    (c) Unassessed waste.

- Other *porambokes*, if available, Panchayat can utilize with the sanction of the District Collector.
- Income from 2C *patta* will go to Panchayat.
- In future no 2C *patta* will be issued without the consent of Panchayat.

- Trees belonging to Highways Department standing on road margins will be leased to Panchayat on five years' average.
- Withered and wind fallen trees of Highways Department to be auctioned by the Department and full amount to be credited to Panchayat deducting seignorage fees.
- Panchayat is entitled to usufructs of trees on the beds of PWD irrigation sources and also usufructs of withered and wind fallen trees.
- When natured trees in PWD tanks are cut by the PWD 50 per cent of the value goes to PWD and 50 per cent to Panchayat.
- When trees planted under social forestry are cut 40 per cent of the value goes to the department and 60 per cent to Panchayat.

Protection to the Presidents

1. Panchayat can sue any person for damages, but others cannot sue Panchayat without giving notice in writing at least of 60 days.
2. If the President is to be prosecuted sanction of the Inspector has to be obtained.
3. No suit or legal proceedings will be tenable against the President and officers acting in good faith.
4. Assessment of tax cannot be challenged in court of law.
5. Wrongful resistance to executive authority or his delegates is an offence punishable under section 341G I. P.C.
6. Prohibition against obstruction of Panchayat President, Executive Authority, member or any employee.
7. Prohibition against removal or defacing of notice.
8. Penalty for not giving information or giving false information to the President.

Controlling Authorities

- Appointment of officers to supervise the Panchayat.
- Powers of various inspecting officers of the activities of the different levels of Panchayats.

- Powers of various officers for purposes of control.
- Powers to suspend or cancel the resolutions etc., under the Act after following procedure.
- Emergency powers of the District Collector and the Inspector.
- Power to take action in case of default on Gram Panchayat President or executive authority.
- Power to remove the President who wilfully fails or refuses to carry out the provisions of the Act.
- Removal of defaulting Vice-President.
- Notice of no confidence against the Vice-President of the Panchayat – powers of officers acting on behalf of the Panchayat and liability to pay compensation.
- Dissolution of the Panchayat for committing persistent irregularities.
- Provision for issue of surcharge certificate for causing loss to the Panchayat.
- Power of the Gram Sabha to review and control the activities of the Panchayat.

Leases by Panchayats

Properties of Panchayats that can be leased out :

1. Own lands and buildings.
2. Government *poramboke* lands vested with and regulated by the Panchayats.
3. Right to enjoy usufructs of trees, collection of fees from markets, bus stands, cart stands etc., fishery rights of water sources belonging to the Panchayat.
4. Auction sale of unserviceable articles, old stores, materials, old news papers journals and other articles.

Period of Lease

Fishery lease	–	5 years
Lands and buildings	–	initially renewable for 3 years and can be further renewed for 3 more years with consent of the Panchayat.

Authority to conduct auction of lease or sale

Executive authority duly assisted by a committee consisting of Vice-President and members of wards where the lease properties are located.

Instalments

Number of instalments of payment of auction amount to be fixed taking into consideration the nature of property leased out.

Security Deposit

Security deposit for auction to be fixed considering the previous year lease amount and the probable amount which will be realized by auction.

Preparation of Notice of Auction

Mode of preparation/conditions to be imposed in auction

Right of executive authority to reject any offer at the auction without assigning any reasons.

Failure to follow conditions of lease and non-payment of instalment of lease amount within the fixed time will end in termination of lease.

Publication of Auction Notice

Mode of publication in wards where property is located – in newspapers when the lease amount exceeds prescribed amount.

Intimation to be sent by post to the probable bidders.

Auction Procedure

Auction can be conducted at the site where property is located if the Panchayat so decides.

Auction to be conducted item by item as mentioned in the auction notice.

Besides security deposit, an amount equivalent to the first instalment of lease amount – to be collected as soon as auction is over for an item.

Re-auction

Re-auction can be conducted by the Panchayat if a person comes forward to remit one and a half time the highest bid in the already conducted auction (or) if the lease is terminated in the middle by the violation of conditions by the lessee.

Confirmation

Confirmation to be done in the meeting of the Panchayat.

Lease Deed

To be signed after stipulating the various conditions decided upon in the meeting of the Panchayat.

Auction-cum-Tender Procedure

If two or more bidders join together and bid for a lesser amount, auction-cum-tender procedure can be adopted simultaneously.

First, the auction procedure has to be completed and then tenders are to be opened.

Panchayat can decide on the highest bid amount in the tender or auction and record the reasons for such decision.

Departmental Management

When there is a gap between the termination of lease and the time of re-auction and when the lease is terminated in the middle of the lease period temporary departmental management can be resorted to.

Audit, Disallowance and Damage

Auditors

The Deputy Block Development Officer and the Assistant Director of Panchayat (Audit) are the auditors appointed by the Government for the audit of Gram Panchayat accounts.

Preparing for Audit

The Gram Panchayat shall send the annual accounts of the Panchayat as soon as the financial year is over and not later than 31st May to the Deputy Block Development Officer/Assistant Director (Audit).

All the prescribed registers are to be written and completed.

The Gram Panchayat President shall verify whether there are vouchers and sanction of the Panchayat for every item of expenditure.

He shall also satisfy himself that all the items of income for which receipts are given are accounted for in the cash book and the pass book.

Functions of Auditor

He shall verify the following items on the receipt side :

1. Whether all taxes to be levied have been levied properly.
2. Whether there is any leakage of revenue.
3. Whether all the licence fees and other fees leviable under the Act have been levied.
4. Whether the grants or resources due from government have been realised.
5. Whether all the leases and auctions have been conducted in time and whether there is any loss due to delay.
6. Whether all the amounts collected by the Panchayat have been properly accounted for.
7. Whether there are any irregularities in the collection and remittance.
8. Whether the write-offs and remissions are proper.
9. Whether reconciliation has been done between the cash book and the pass book.

On the expenditure side he shall verify the following items :

1. Availability of vouchers for all items of expenditure.
2. Whether there are any irregular or inadmissible expenditures.
3. Whether there are any avoidable expenditures.
4. Whether there is any defalcation in expenditure.

5. Whether the prescribed procedure has been followed in purchase.
6. Whether stock entries have been made for all the purchases.
7. Whether prescribed procedure has been followed in contract and execution of works.

Procedure to be followed after the receipt of the Audit Report

Replies to all audit reports and objections have to be prepared by the President of the Gram Panchayat within two months of receipt of the audit report.

The audit report and the replies are to be placed in the Panchayat meeting and approval to be obtained.

The audit report and replies are to be put up in the Gram Sabha meeting of the Panchayat.

Scrutiny of replies by the Deputy Block Development Officer

The Deputy Block Development Officer will peruse the replies submitted by the Gram Panchayat and with his recommendations submit it to the Assistant Director (Audit) for settlement.

Orders of Assistant Director (Audit)

The Assistant Director (Audit) shall settle all the audit objections on the basis of the replies submitted by the Gram Panchayat President.

Surcharge Notice

For serious audit objections involving financial irregularities for which the replies furnished are not satisfactory, the Assistant Director (Audit) will issue surcharge notice to the concerned Gram Panchayat President who committed the serious irregularities.

Surcharge Certificate

If the replies furnished by the President to the surcharge notice are not satisfactory the Assistant Director (Audit) will issue surcharge certificate against the President for recovery of the loss incurred from him.

Procedure of Appeal

The President shall appeal to the District Collector if the surcharge certificate issued against him.

The next appeal shall lie to the Government.

A final appeal can be made to the High Court.

Planning

1. Necessity of Planning
2. Formation of Planning Committee in each Panchayat with the following members:

    1. Members of Panchayat
    2. Teachers
    3. Experienced Elders
    4. Youth interested in development
    5. Department officers.

3. Steps in Planning

    1. Collection of basic statistics from

        (i) Census
        (ii) DISNIC through NIC
        (iii) Director of Statistics
        (iv) BPL Survey Details
        (v) Details from other development departments
        (vi) Basic statistics from Gram Panchayat
        (vii) Panchayat resource information fed in computers.

    2. Verification of basic statistics and resources in the field.
    3. Resource Mapping Benchmark Survey

        (i) Natural resources
        (ii) Human resources

(iii) Available infrastructure
(iv) Various types of industries available and their present status.

4. Field verification of resources through the method of participatory rural appraisal.
5. Marking of resources in the village map.
6. To assess individual family income, collection of family income and expenditure details and consolidating them at village level.
7. Preparation of village profile in all hamlets

   (i) Population
   (ii) Family Census
   (iii) Agriculture and Animal Husbandry
   (iv) Industries
   (v) Drinking Water Sources
   (vi) Streetlights
   (vii) Link Roads
   (viii) Public Health
   (ix) Public Distribution
   (x) Water Resources
   (xi) Infrastructure available

8. Identification of problems and requirements through seminars

   (i) Conduct of meeting of Planning Committee.
   (ii) Discussion of gap between existing facilities and requirements.
   (iii) Estimating rough cost of expenditure.
   (iv) Discussion of departmental schemes.

9. Identification of development disparities and preparation of plan without bias.
10. Preparation of plan requirements through discussion in Gram Sabha meeting.
11. Preparation of shelf of project for 10 years.
12. Finding resources for plan implementation

(i) From State Government schemes,
(ii) From Central Government schemes,
(iii) From Gram Panchayat schemes.

13. Finding ways to augment resources for plan implementation

(i) Infrastructure loans, (HUDCO),
(ii) Bank loan,
(iii) Funds from NGOs,
(iv) Public contribution.

14. Preparation of Gram Panchayat development plan

(i) For individual family benefit schemes,
(ii) For community development schemes,
(iii) Integration of departmental schemes.

15. Gram Sabha and Panchayat

The Gram Panchayat plans prepared shall be approved by the Gram Sabha and the Gram Panchayat.

16. Sending of plan to the Panchayat Union

The Gram Panchayat plan prepared shall be sent to the Panchayat Union concerned for consolidation and forwarding to the District Panchayat and the District Planning Committee.

Gram Sabha

1. Constituted as per Article 243(A) of the 73rd Constitution Amendment Act.
2. Formed as per Section 3 of the Tamil Nadu Panchayats Act, 1996.
3. *Members* – All the electors in the Gram Panchayat are members.

4. *Place and date of meeting* - Common place in the panchayat limits and date fixed by Gram Panchayat.
5. *Meeting Notice* - Seven days in advance of date of meeting and subjects as approved in Gram Panchayat meeting shall be included in the notice.
6. Publicity through tom-tom, bit notices in Panchayat office, school buildings, overhead tanks etc.
7. Meeting notices to be sent to the Inspector seven days in advance.
8. *Quorum* - Ten per cent of number of persons in the electoral roll of the Panchayat.
9. Adjournment - If the required quorum of members do not turn up within half an hour fixed for the conduct of the meeting it can be adjourned.
10. The President shall maintain full control over the conduct of meeting.
11. *Observer* - The District Collector shall send a nodal officer as an observer to assist the President in the conduct of meeting.
12. *Attendance Register and Minutes Book* - The signature of persons who attended the meeting shall be obtained and all the discussions and decisions thereon shall be recorded in a minutes book.
13. *Submission to Inspector* - Within 72 hours of conduct of meeting minutes small be sent to the Inspector.

Subjects to be Included

1. Approval of list of beneficiaries selected by the village.
2. Approval of sites selected for construction of buildings.
3. Review of works executed by the Gram Panchayat President in the previous year and scrutiny of list of works implemented by other departments.
4. Promotion of communal harmony among various communities.
5. Collection of contribution in kind or cash for community development schemes.
6. Approval of Gram Panchayat Budget, Accounts and Audit reports.

Dates of meeting of Gram Sabha fixed by Government

1st May, 15th August, 2nd October, 26th January

Expenditure for Gram Sabha Meeting

An expenditure of Rs.500 (five hundred) is allowed from Panchayat funds for Gram Sabha meeting.

- Powers of the Gram Sabha – Section 3(3).
- Additional powers given to the Gram Sabha – GO Rg. No.152 dated 20-7-1998.

Explaining the implications of powers of the Gram Sabha

What are the additional matters which can be discussed by the Gram Sabha and decisions taken in the interest of the people.

1. Ensuring 100 per cent enrolment of school age children.
2. Preservation of environment sanitation.
3. Water management.
4. Rain water harvest – improvement of ground water potential.
5. PDS – better distribution and weeding out bogus cards.
6. Tree planting and increasing forest area.
7. Pollution control.
8. Proper exploitation of natural resources.
9. Preservation of natural resources.
10. Public properties – proper maintenance, removal of encroachment.
11. Flood control measures.
12. Improving resources by Panchayat.
13. Improving collection of Panchayat target fees.
14. Vermi compost – encouragement and development.
15. Small family norms.
16. Small savings, health development.
17. Night patrol of rural areas.
18. Offences – watching and prevention.
19. Vegetable gardens for nutrition – medicinal plants growing.
20. Eradication of illicit arrack.
21. Voluntary labour – encouragement.
22. Eliminating human rights violation.

23. Proper utilization of amenities and facilities.
24. Eradication of corruption.
25. Encouraging public participation in village meetings.

Social Development

Total Sanitation

- What is sanitation?
- What is total sanitation?
- Why Sanitation?
- Concept – explanation.
- Needed facilities for sanitation.
- Needed conditions for sanitation.
- Condition of the village in terms of sanitation.
- Comparison of our position with the worst.
- Linkage between sanitation and development.
- Poor sanitation and its implications.
- Prevailing common diseases in the rural areas.

Introduction

1. Status of sanitation in rural India compared with that in the developed nations.
2. Death rate due to poor sanitation.
3. Types and characteristics of poor sanitation.
4. Prevailing common diseases and reasons in the context of poor sanitation.
5. The role of human resources development in socio-economic development of nation.

Seven Components of Rural Sanitation

1. Safe handling of drinking water.
2. Safe disposal of sewage water.
3. Safe disposal of human excreta.
4. Safe disposal of solid waste.
5. Maintaining personal hygiene.
6. Maintaining environment at home and cleanliness of food.
7. Maintaining the village environment.

The participants have been oriented in the above components targeting individual, family, and village community in total. The role and responsibility of the Gram Panchayat administration in implementing this scheme in their area have been explained. They have been sensitized on utilization of facilities to achieve development. It has been indicated that the leaders should make sanitation a culture rather than implement the scheme. Case studies of successful model Panchayats have been explained.

Implementation Procedure of Sanitation Programme

In the total rural sanitation programme funds are earmarked for the following activities in each village :

- Construction of individual toilets – with an incentive of Rs.500 to 600 per toilet.
- School toilet – permission is given for the renovation of old toilets and also new construction could be done under this scheme – Rs.20,000 for construction of new toilet in schools.
- Toilet in *balwadi* – can be designed for the convenience of children, and the earmarked fund is Rs.6000.
- Rural sanitary mart – where the various materials of sanitation will be available to serve groups of Gram Panchayats. The sanitary mart should be located in a roadside area so that transportation of concerned materials is easy – Panchayat may also operate these marts.
- Women's sanitary complex – SHG has to take the responsibility of operation and maintenance of the complex.
- Those village Panchayats which promptly and successfully implement the above activities of the scheme will be given priority in the allocation of other development schemes.
- Community organizations and institutional building under the scheme – village sanitation committee has to be organized and should be strengthened.

For effective IEC activities, a benchmark survey has to be undertaken. Mass awareness, dissemination of various components of the scheme, mass propaganda through both print and electronic media has to be carried out. Publishing of posters, hand bills, stickers, banners, organization of exhibition in schools and public places have to be planned and the role of the Gram Panchayat in IEC activities has been explained.

Gender Sensitization

The concept of gender, sex and gender equality have been explained. They have been briefed about the condition of women in India particularly in the rural areas and how ameliorative measures can be taken in this regard.

Group Discussion

Status of sanitation in a village was given for group discussion and the participants were asked to visualize the best model village and to prepare an action plan on how they were going to make use of the TRSP in their village. After the discussion all group leaders were asked to present their reports. All the group leaders presented their reports.

Conscientization of the Leaders on

(a) The status and position of women in India, particularly in Tamil Nadu.
(b) The problems faced by the women in home, society, economy and polity.
(c) Position of girl child in Indian society, particularly in the rural areas.
(d) Laws and decisions to protect the girl child and women.
(e) Provision in Panchayat to work for upliftment of women.
(f) Differentiating sex from gender.
(g) Gender equality and equity.
(h) Organized power of women.
(i) Building the skill and capability of women.
(j) Building the skill and capability of women leaders
(k) Building alliance for women's empowerment.
(l) Pre-natal and post-natal care.

Creating Awareness among Leaders on Computer Utility

(a) Facilities available in the computer.
(b) How it can be used for rural development?
(c) How to get information from the computer?
(d) How accounts can be maintained in the computer?
(e) How profitably the computer can be utilized in Panchayats?

On Leadership

A full session was devoted to building leadership qualities by Dr. G. Palanithurai wherein he indicated the following essential qualities of a leader :

- Leader will be a role model.
- Leader will change the environment.
- Leader will have a can-do attitude.
- Leader will have commitment.
- Leader will have faith in himself/herself.
- Leader will have faith in people.
- Leader will have needed capacity.
- Leader will have patience.
- Leader will have perseverance.
- Leader will have endurance.
- Leader will be on the side of solution and not a part of the problem.
- Leader will be an inevitable person.
- Leader will have humanism.
- Leader is not an individual but an institution and a movement.
- Leader will have goals, plan and target.
- Leader will have resoluteness.
- Leader will have a vision and a mission.
- Leader will enjoy difficulties.
- Leader will like challenges and respond to challenges.
- Leader will convert every challenge into an opportunity.

Role Model

Koothampakkam Gram Panchayat President Mr. Elango fielded a session and explained to the participants his struggle and indicated the road map to achieve success in Panchayat administration. It was very useful for them as he suggested that sharing among the Panchayat Presidents will help Panchayat leaders to gain confidence. He has given a name to it, namely, "Panchayats to Panchayats". By coming together Panchayat leaders can achieve many things. He further said that Panchayat leaders can come together as a block for generating economic activities. He explained the innovative practices of Gram Panchayat Presidents. In each batch one role model Panchayat President was identified and she/he was asked to share her/his experience in Panchayat administration. Of all the sessions, this session was more interesting to the participants as they received information from the horse's mouth.

Special Session

There are certain gray areas in Panchayats and to explain the issues in those areas, special classes were arranged. Mr. N.S. Chidambaram usually took these classes between 6:00 and 8:30 p.m. It was not a regular class. This arrangement was based on the demand of the Panchayati Presidents. It was not compulsory. Yet, 80 per cent of the trainees attended this programme. This is the indicator of the interest evinced by the Panchayat Presidents in the training programme. This is the new programme introduced voluntarily by Mr. N.S. Chidambaram without asking for any remuneration. It was responded to very well by the trainees.

Experts from the Departments of Environment, Women Empowerment and Human Rights held discussions with the Panchayat Presidents. The discussions were not part of the regular time-table. Whenever they were free they used to come to the training spot and interact with the Presidents. Sometimes they did so at night since the programme was residential. They also provided reading material to the Presidents. Government officials working in sectoral departments had been asked to visit the training spot and interact with the Presidents about their activities in the rural areas. All this happened because of the initiative of the District Collectors.

Inputs for Behavioural Change (Women)

Everyday Ms. Uma, (Coordinator for training the women), separately before the starting of the regular sessions briefed the elected women representatives about the change looked forward to their behaviour. How to keep the rooms, the bathrooms and the toilets clean, how to sit in a classroom and how to behave in a crowd, how to interact with officials, how to ask questions in the classroom, how to speak on a platform were discussed with the elected women representatives by Ms. Uma. She was always with the representatives, discussing with them the new culture that had to be inculcated. Many of the elected women representatives did not have toilet facilities in their houses and they do not know how to use the toilets. Uma told them how to use the toilets. Many of the women representatives were in the habit of chewing tobacco and Uma told them that leaders should refrain from using the tobacco.

Trainees Expectation

The elected women representatives belonging to different socio-economic categories and their educational background also varied. Hence their perceptions vary from individual to individual. They needed information, skill and supportive structure as they perceived that their capability to tackle officials was limited. They need continuous training. They required continuous support from the training institute. To clear their doubts, periodical meetings could be arranged at the District Collector's office under the chairmanship of the District Collector. Their doubts and problems could then be sorted out by the officials.

Briefing about the Women Federation

Ms. Uma, used to ask the women Panchayat leaders what they needed for your effective functioning. They wanted institutional and organisational help for their sustained activities. Of course, training gave confidence skill and information and it raised hope. But when they started their work in the Panchayat they had to face a volley of problems and tried to solve them. But at some point of time they lost heart and hope as anti-social elements in the panchayat area disturbed their activities. At such times the women leaders needed the support of Gandhigram Rural Institute particularly The Hunger Project Unit. Ms. Uma explained to them the major achievements of the federation of women panchayat leaders and asked them to enroll themselves as members. The majority of them were willing to enrol themselves as members. Ms. Uma gave them the mailing address of the federation leaders.

Consultation

The trainees had individual local, specific, peculiar problems and issues for which they required advice, solutions and remedies. These issues could not be raised in the classroom. Hence they used to contact the experts who were staying in the Guest House for consultation. For each and every case the experts gave suggestions by referring to the Act, GOs and rules. This exercise took place during the night between 9.00 and 11.00 everyday. This was a good practice. Both the experts and the Panchayat leaders benefited. Experts learnt of unique problems while hearing the individual cases. These issues and problems will be useful for policy advocacy. At the same time Panchayat leaders get correct advice and counselling. In some areas the experts contacted the concerned Block Development officials and informed them about the rules. Thus officials got their mistakes corrected also.

Behaviour of the Trainees

Of the trainees, women were attentive, responsive, sincere, eager to learn and open to advice. From morning till evening and even in special sessions, all the women representatives were present. Among men 70 per cent were attentive, sincere and attended with a sense of commitment. But 30 per cent of the male trainees tried to while away the time. Some of them were not disciplined and as a result they disturbed the atmosphere in the hostel. Somehow they were all managed. But a special session was devoted to discuss the attitudinal change and behavioural change.

All the women representatives were regular in attending the classes. They were always punctual. They were open to learn. All of them attended the special sessions in the night. They have gained enormous amount of information as they have realized that they have not adequately established their grip over Panchayat administration. They regulate themselves in the hostels while staying in the hostels. Women leaders who participated in the training programme used to attend the valedictory programme along with men leaders. In the valedictory programme the elected women representatives gave their feedback about the training programme they used to initiate the men and other politicians in the podiums. Unfortunately the men used to laugh at them. Sometimes they used to clap. The elected women representatives had developed confidence and spoke in the programme on par with men leaders. One important thing among the women leaders is that they consider the space available in the Panchayat institutions is meant for development not for politics.

Material Provided

A manual compiled by Dr. G. Palanithurai entitled, *New Panchayat Raj System in Tamil Nadu: Act, Rules and Schemes* was provided to them. The 763 page manual consists of the updated Tamil Nadu Panchayati Act, 84 Government Orders (Rules) pertaining to Gram Panchayat Administration, current rural development schemes of both Centre and State Governments. Apart from this manual, a small guide with details of roles, responsibilities, duties, powers of the Gram Panchayat was provided to each and every trainee for easy understanding of the system. Further a small folder entitled "Charter of Panchayat" was also given to them. A nicely designed jute bag, a scripling pad with a Reynolds pen were provided.

Small Tips

How to read the Act, Government orders and rules is the major question haunting the minds of many of the Presidents. Someone openly asked the resource person Mr. Chidambaram in the session how to read the book. He took about 15 minutes to explain the details. Likewise how to address the problems through letters to officials was explained. The methodology of writing such letters was also explained.

Nature of Training

Totally it was a residential training, KVK, Gandhigram, was the venue for the training. Participants and resource persons stayed in the hostels and the Guest House, respectively. It provided opportunity for both resource persons and participants to have closer interaction. Further many of the trainees wanted special class on certain aspects of Panchayat administration. It was possible as it was a fully residential training programme. Moreover documentary films on Panchayats were shown only after 8.30 p.m. everyday.

Methodology

In all the sessions, the trainers used to deliver lectures on the subject given to them. After the lecture, there was a discussion on the lecture. Following the general lectures, focused lectures were arranged and discussed very intensively the subjects. On many of the issues, Panchayat Presidents were grouped and subjects were given to these groups who were asked them to come out with solutions. The whole exercise was in participatory mode. In every batch a role model leader was identified and the other participants were asked to speak to the leaders about their experience.

Material Used

In all the classes, overhead projector was provided. Charts were used more in number for women leaders. Documentary films were shown to them in the night. For each and every subject printed material was provided.

Field Visit

Field visits were arranged on the last day of the programme. Time was very short. Only a few Presidents could visit all the production units of Gandhigram Trust. Gandhigram has many small industries producing medicines, soaps, shampoo, ragi malt, napkin and a number of other articles. Some of the Presidents stayed back and visited these units the next day.

About Logistics

Generally arrangements are good. Classrooms have adequate space and ventilation. It was comfortable. But the Panchayat Presidents with varied age groups found it very difficult to sit through out the day. They did not have such a practice in their life. They said that their absorbing capacity, and reflecting capacity are poor. As the information supplied by the resource person are useful and interesting, the Panchayat Presidents sat althrough in the class. Simple accommodation was given and that too in the hostel. Rich vegetarian food was given. Panchayat Presidents demanded non-vegetarian food. As it is a Gandhian Institution, only vegetarian food was provided.

Socio-Economic Background (Men)

Table 1 : Distribution of Respondents by Age

Sl. No.	Category	PUD		DGL		TRH		SIV		RAM		THE		KAR		VIRD		Total	%
		N	%	N	%	N	%	N	%	N	%	N	%	N	%	N	%		
1.	Up to 25	15	54	11	6.2	52	20.3	14	7.5	41	17.9	4	6.1	9	10.6	39	15.9	185	12.1
2.	25 to 35	90	32.3	65	36.5	86	33.6	24	12.8	36	15.7	8	12.1	14	16.5	38	15.5	361	23.7
3.	36 to 45	92	33.0	61	34.3	71	27.7	64	34.0	56	24.5	16	24.2	16	18.8	87	35.5	463	30.3
4.	46 +	82	29.3	41	23.0	47	18.4	86	45.7	96	41.9	38	57.6	40	54.1	81	33.1	517	33.9
	Total	279	100	178	100	256	100	188	100	229	100	66	100	85	100	245	100	1526	100

Source: Computed.

Of the 1526, 12 per cent belong to the youngest category. 54 per cent of the respondents belong to the age group between 25 and 45. The rest belong to the 46 years and above category. The majority of the respondents belong to neither the old age group nor the youngest one.

Table 2 : Distribution of Respondents by Education

Sl. No.	Category	PUD		DGL		TRH		SIV		RAM		THE		KAR		VIRD		Total	%
		N	%	N	%	N	%	N	%	N	%	N	%	N	%	N	%		
1.	Illiterate	–	–	7	3.9	–	–	3	1.59	3	1.3	–	–	1	1.2	7	2.9	21	1.4
2.	Primary	63	22.5	38	21.3	59	23.0	28	14.89	37	16.2	11	16.7	12	14.1	81	33.1	329	21.6
3.	Secondary	145	52	93	52.3	121	47.3	35	18.6	52	22.7	21	31.8	19	22.4	66	26.9	552	36.2
4.	Higher Secondary	20	7.2	22	12.4	18	7.0	85	46.24	109	47.6	16	24.2	41	48.2	74	30.2	385	25.2
5.	Degree or Post-Graduate	51	18.3	13	7.3	52	20.3	33	17.55	24	10.5	17	25.8	10	11.8	14	5.7	214	14.0
6.	Others	–	–	5	2.8	6	2.4	4	2.1	4	1.7	1	1.5	2	2.3	3	1.2	25	1.6
	Total	279	100	178	100	256	100	188	100	229	100	66	100	85	100	245	100	1526	100

Source: Computed.

Of the total participants, 83 per cent are having sound educational background (schooling) to manage the panchayats. Only 1.4 per cent are illiterates while 14 per cent of them are having graduation as their educational background.

Table 3 : Distribution of Respondents by Religion

Sl. No.	Category	PUD		DGL		TRH		SIV		RAM		THE		KAR		VIRD		Total	%
		N	%	N	%	N	%	N	%	N	%	N	%	N	%	N	%		
1.	Hindu	259	92.8	169	94.9	243	94.9	183	97.3	218	93.5	66	100	5	100	24	85.8	1464	95.9
2.	Christian	13	4.7	8	4.5	7	2.8	3	1.6	9	3.9	-	-	-	-	2	7.1	42	2.8
3.	Muslim	7	2.5	1	0.6	6	2.3	2	1.1	2	2.6	-	-	-	-	2	7.1	20	1.3
	Total	279	100	178	100	256	100	188	100	229	100	66	100	5	100	28	100	1526	100

Source: Computed.

Of the total respondents, 95.9 per cent belong to the Hindu religion, while 2.8 per cent and 1.3 per cent of the respondents belong to Christianity and Islam respectively.

Table 4 : Distribution of Respondents by Community

Sl. No.	Community	PUD		DGL		TRH		SIV		RAM		THE		KAR		VIRD		Total	%
		N	%	N	%	N	%	N	%	N	%	N	%	N	%	N	%		
1.	SC	53	19.1	41	23.0	48	18.8	37	19.7	56	24.5	9	13.7	18	21.2	62	25.3	324	21.2
2.	BC	151	54.1	99	55.6	142	55.5	97	51.6	113	49.3	29	43.9	22	25.9	102	41.6	755	49.6
3.	MBC	63	22.5	38	21.4	54	21.1	49	26.1	54	23.6	28	42.4	35	41.2	81	33.1	402	26.3
4.	OC	12	4.3	-	-	12	4.6	5	2.65	6	2.6	-	-	10	1.8	-	-	45	2.9
	Total	279	100	178	100	256	100	188	100	229	100	66	100	85	100	245	100	1526	100

Source: Computed.

Of the respondents, 21.2 per cent belong to SC, 49.6 per cent belong to BC and 26.3 per cent belong to MBC. Only 2.9 per cent of the respondents having from forward communities. So 97 per cent of the representatives belonging to the downtrodden categories. It is a reality that power has gone to the poorest segment also because of the reservation introduced in the Panchayat Raj System.

Table 5 : Distribution of Respondents by Occupation

Sl. No.	Occupation	PUD		DGL		TRH		SIV		RAM		THE		KAR		VIRD		Total	%
		N	%	N	%	N	%	N	%	N	%	N	%	N	%	N	%		
1.	Agriculture	217	77.7	152	85.4	225	87.9	158	84.1	208	90.8	49	74.2	41	48.2	162	66.1	1212	79.4
2.	Coolie	30	10.8	15	8.4	-	-	4	2.1	6	2.6	7	10.6	-	-	31	12.7	93	6.1
3.	Business	32	11.5	5	2.8	15	5.9	13	6.92	12	5.2	2	3.0	25	29.4	16	6.5	120	7.9
4.	Others	-	-	6	3.4	7	2.7	12	6.38	3	1.4	3	4.6	9	10.6	32	13.1	72	4.7
5.	Contract work	-	-	-	-	5	2.0	-	-	-	-	-	-	-	-	-	-	5	0.3
6.	Lawyers	-	-	-	-	4	1.5	-	-	-	-	-	-	-	-	-	-	4	0.3
7.	Private Employee	-	-	-	-	-	-	1	0.5	-	-	5	7.6	10	11.8	4	1.6	20	1.3
	Total	279	100	178	100	256	100	188	100	229	100	66	100	85	100	245	100	1526	100

Source: Computed.

It is beyond doubt that power in the rural areas in the hands of the agriculturists. 79 per cent of the respondents belong to agricultural family and farming is the major source of activities while 6 per cent are coolie and 7.9 per cent are businessmen (small business).

Table 6 : Distribution of Respondents by Landholdings

Sl. No.	Land (in acres)	PUD		DGL		TRH		SIV		RAM		THE		KAR		VIRD		Total	%
		N	%	N	%	N	%	N	%	N	%	N	%	N	%	N	%		
1.	No land	22	7.9	17	9.6	21	8.2	23	12.2	16	7.0	4	6.1	6	7.1	83	33.9	192	12.6
2.	Upto 3 acres	169	6.6	105	59.0	138	53.9	92	48.9	147	64.2	31	47.4	8	9.4	48	29.6	73	48.4
3.	3 to 5 acres	46	16.3	38	21.3	76	29.7	30	16.0	58	25.3	17	25.8	25	21.4	59	36.4	349	22.8
4.	5 and above	42	15.0	18	10.1	21	8.2	43	22.9	8	3.5	14	21.2	46	54.1	55	34.0	247	16.2
	Total	279	100	178	100	256	100	188	100	229	100	66	100	85	100	245	100	1526	100

Source: Computed.

Of the respondents, 71 per cent are small farmers having lands up to five acres; 12.6 per cent do not have lands, and 16.2 per cent of the respondents own more than five acres of land.

Table 7 : Distribution of Respondents by Type of Family

Sl. No.	Category	PUD		DGL		TRH		SIV		RAM		THE		KAR		VIRD		Total	%
		N	%	N	%	N	%	N	%	N	%	N	%	N	%	N	%		
1.	Nuclear	172	61.6	118	66.3	168	65.6	89	47.4	119	52.0	40	60.6	49	57.6	174	71.0	929	60.9
2.	Joint	107	38.4	60	33.7	88	34.4	99	52.6	110	48.0	26	39.4	36	42.4	71	29.0	597	39.1
	Total	279	100	178	100	256	100	188	100	229	100	66	100	85	100	245	100	1526	100

Source: Computed.

It is curious to note that 60.9 per cent of the representatives are in nuclear families while 39.1 per cent are in joint families.

Table 8 : Distribution of Respondents by Type of Housing

Sl. No.	Housing Pattern	PUD		DGL		TRH		SIV		RAM		THE		KAR		VIRD		Total	%
		N	%	N	%	N	%	N	%	N	%	N	%	N	%	N	%		
1.	Huts	74	26.5	12	6.7	8	3.2	10	5.31	6	2.7	7	10.6	14	16.5	6	2.4	137	9.0
2.	Tiled	108	38.7	94	52.8	126	49.2	102	54.3	157	68.5	23	34.8	41	48.2	109	44.5	760	49.8
3.	Pucca	67	24.0	61	34.3	106	41.4	63	33.5	57	24.9	29	43.9	24	28.2	114	49.4	521	34.1
4.	Colony	11	3.9	5	2.8	7	2.7	7	3.74	4	1.7	2	3.0	3	3.5	9	3.7	48	3.2
5.	Rent	19	6.8	6	3.4	9	3.5	6	3.7	5	2.2	5	7.7	3	3.5	7	2.9	60	3.9
	Total	279	100	178	100	256	100	188	100	229	100	66	100	85	100	245	100	1526	100

Source: Computed.

34.1 per cent of the respondents have their own *pucca* houses; 9 per cent of them are living in huts; 3.2 per cent are living in colony houses; 3.9 per cent of the representatives are living in rented buildings, and 49.8 per cent live in tiled houses.

Table 9 : Distribution of Respondents by Possessing of Electricity Facility

Sl. No.	Electricity Facility	PUD		DGL		TRH		SIV		RAM		THE		KAR		VIRD		Total	%
		N	%	N	%	N	%	N	%	N	%	N	%	N	%	N	%		
1.	Yes	239	85.7	168	94.4	238	93.0	181	96.3	226	98.7	63	95.5	81	95.3	238	97.7	1434	94.0
2.	No	40	14.3	10	5.6	18	7.0	7	3.7	3	1.3	3	4.5	4	4.7	7	2.9	92	6.0
	Total	279	100	178	100	256	100	188	100	229	100	66	100	85	100	245	100	1526	100

Source: Computed

Nearly 94 per cent of the respondents have electricity connection to their houses while 6 per cent of the respondents do not have such facility in their houses.

Table 10 : Distribution of Respondents by Possessing of Toilet Facility

Sl. No.	Toilet Facility	PUD		DGL		TRH		SIV		RAM		THE		KAR		VIRD		Total	%
		N	%	N	%	N	%	N	%	N	%	N	%	N	%	N	%		
1.	Yes	126	45.2	104	58.4	154	60.2	96	51.1	169	73.8	38	57.6	56	65.9	162	66.1	905	59.3
2.	No	153	54.8	74	41.6	102	39.8	92	48.9	60	26.2	28	42.4	29	34.1	83	33.9	621	40.7
	Total	279	100	178	100	256	100	188	100	229	100	66	100	85	100	245	100	1526	100

Source: Computed.

The Government of Tamil Nadu is planning to implement the total rural sanitation programme through the Gram Panchayats. While 59 per cent of the respondents have toilet facilities in their houses, 41 per cent of the leaders do not have such facilities in their houses. The panchayat leader should set up a model to the others. Since 30 to 40 per cent of the panchayat leaders are poor, they may not be able to have such facility. Now thanks to the government, they will have such facilities in their houses.

Table 11 : Distribution of Respondents by Possessing of Water Tap Connection Facility

Sl. No.	Tap Connection	PUD		DGL		TRH		SIV		RAM		THE		KAR		VIRD		Total	%
		N	%	N	%	N	%	N	%	N	%	N	%	N	%	N	%		
1.	Yes	73	26.2	57	32.0	197	77.0	70	37.2	58	25.3	27	40.9	47	55.3	108	44.1	637	41.7
2.	No	206	73.8	121	68.0	59	23.0	118	62.8	171	74.7	39	59.1	38	44.7	137	55.9	889	58.3
	Total	279	100	178	100	256	100	188	100	229	100	66	100	85	100	245	100	1526	100

Source: Computed.

Individual water tap connection is being provided in the Panchayat area after getting a deposit amount from the individual. Further they have to pay water charges regularly. In the case of the Panchayat Presidents nearly 58 per cent of them do not have such facilities in their houses while 42 per cent of the respondents have such facilities in their houses.

Table 12 : Details of Family Members of the Respondent

Sl. No.	Family members	PUD		DGL		TRH		SIV		RAM		THE		KAR		VIRD		Total	%
		N	%	N	%	N	%	N	%	N	%	N	%	N	%	N	%		
1.	Two	16	5.7	25	14.0	13	5.1	7	3.72	3	1.3	3	7.6	4	4.7	5	2.0	78	5.1
2.	Three	56	20.1	33	18.6	28	10.9	24	12.76	18	7.9	6	9.1	9	10.6	59	24.1	233	15.3
3.	Four	68	24.4	49	27.5	48	18.8	18	9.57	30	13.1	9	13.6	22	25.9	67	27.4	31	21.4
4.	Five	128	32.3	41	23.0	31	12.1	21	11.17	47	20.5	13	19.7	18	21.2	78	31.8	377	24.7
5.	More than five	11	3.9	30	16.9	136	53.1	118	62.75	131	59.2	33	50.0	32	37.6	36	14.7	527	34.5
	Total	279	100	178	100	256	100	188	100	229	100	66	100	85	100	245	100	1526	100

Source: Computed.

Of the respondents, 34.5 per cent have more than five family members. A family norm is being fixed through an Act for an individual to qualify to contest in the election and subsequently the Act is validated through judgement. But the Tamil Nadu Local Body representatives will be found to have crossed the well established norm.

Table 13 : Party Affiliation of the Respondent

Sl. No.	Party	PUD		DGL		TRH		SIV		RAM		THE		KAR		VIRD		Total	%
		N	%	N	%	N	%	N	%	N	%	N	%	N	%	N	%		
1.	AIADMK	45	41.2	56	31.5	94	36.7	69	51.8	85	53.7	32	48.5	37	54.5	127	61.7	615	40.3
2.	DMK	70	25.1	49	27.5	92	35.9	28	21.1	47	29.7	13	22.0	19	27.9	60	29.1	378	24.8
3.	Congress I	27	9.7	23	13.0	16	6.3	22	16.57	14	8.9	2	3.4	8	11.8	9	4.4	121	7.9
4.	CPI (M)	1	0.4	3	1.7	–	–	9	6.7	4	2.5	2	3.4	2	2.9	3	1.5	24	1.6
5.	MDMK	11	3.9	1	0.6	12	4.7	3	2.25	4	2.5	2	3.4	2	2.9	5	2.3	40	2.6
6.	No party	49	17.5	46	25.8	42	16.4	2	1.6	2	1.3	1	1.7	–	–	2	1.0	348	23.0

Source: Computed.

In Tamil Nadu, Gram Panchayat President's position is not contested on party lines. So, through panchayat presidents, however, affiliate themselves with some political party, they do not act in accordance with the party as they are more interested in responding to the community. Of the total number of presidents, who attended the training programme, 23 per cent did not have any political affiliation. But all the others are affiliated with both national and ethnic political parties.

Table 14 : Distribution of Respondents by Newspaper Reading Habits

Sl. No.	Paper	PUD		DGL		TRH		SIV		RAM		THE		KAR		VIRD		Total	%
		N	%	N	%	N	%	N	%	N	%	N	%	N	%	N	%		
1.	Daily Thanthi	172	29.3	39	29.3	143	55.9	73	32.9	102	19.7	32	21.4	58	15.9	86	26.7	738	25.2
2.	Dinamalar	184		84	34.1	109	42.6	92	35.8	171	33.1	36	19.0	67	18.4	84	26.1	827	28.3
3.	Dinamakaran	33	13.4	33	13.4	25	9.8	21	8.17	53	10.2	–	–	22	6.0	37	11.5	224	7.7
4.	Dinamani	97	6.9	17	6.9	43	16.8	13	5.01	91	17.5	27	16.7	39	10.7	21	6.5	348	11.9
5.	Dinaboomi	42	4.9	12	4.9	2	0.8	6	2.4	24	4.6	18	10.7	–	–	27	8.4	131	4.5
6.	Other papers	68	11.4	28	11.4	–	25	12.1	–	–	–	–	–	–	–	–	–	121	4.1
7.	Malaimalar	–	–	–	–	11	4.3	–	–	–	–	–	–	17	4.7	9	2.8	37	1.3
8.	Indian Express	5	–	–	–	9	3.5	–	–	5	1.0	6	3.6	4	1.1	–	–	25	0.9
9.	Murasoli	72	–	–	–	3	1.2	–	–	–	–	–	–	19	5.2	–	–	94	3.2
10.	The Hindu	8	–	–	–	3	1.2	–	–	–	–	2	1.2	–	–	–	–	13	0.4
11.	Kalaikathir	–	–	–	–	2	0.8	–	–	–	–	–	–	12	3.4	–	–	14	0.4
12.	Employment Guide	–	–	–	–	1	0.4	–	–	–	–	–	–	–	–	–	–	1	0.03
13.	Theekathir	–	–	–	–	–	–	1	0.4	13	2.5	6	3.6	18	4.9	7	2.2	45	1.5
14.	Tamilarasu	6	–	–	–	–	–	6	2.35	–	–	15	8.9	32	8.8	–	–	59	2.0
15.	Malaimurasu	–	–	–	–	–	–	4	1.6	47	9.1	6	3.6	38	10.4	–	–	95	4.3

(Contd.)

Table 14 (Contd.)

Sl. No.	Paper	PUD		DGL		TRH		SIV		RAM		THE		KAR		VIRD		Total	%
		N	%	N	%	N	%	N	%	N	%	N	%	N	%	N	%		
16.	Namathu MGR	32	–	–	–	–	–	–	–	12	2.3	11	6.5	29	8.0	42	13.0	12.6	4.3
17.	Malaimani	–	–	–	–	–	–	–	–	–	–	3	1.8	–	–	–	–	3	0.1
18.	Gramiya Bharath	–	–	–	–	–	–	–	–	–	–	6	3.6	–	–	–	–	6	0.2
19.	Viduthalai	–	–	–	–	–	–	–	–	–	–	–	–	4	1.1	–	–	4	0.1
20.	Janasakthi	–	–	–	–	–	–	–	–	–	–	–	–	5	1.4	–	–	5	0.1
21.	Kathiravan	–	–	–	–	–	–	–	–	–	–	–	–	–	–	9	2.8	9	0.3

Source: Computed.

Gram Panchayat Presidents have the habit of reading newspapers regularly. Nearly 50 per cent of the respondents read *Dinathanthi* and *Dinamalar* regularly. These newspapers are very popular among the people. Others read other newspapers and magazines.

Socio-Economic Background (Women)

Table 15 : Distribution of Respondents by Age Group

Sl. No.	Category	DGL		TRH		PUD		SIV		RAM		THE		KAR		VIRD		Total	%
		N	%	N	%	N	%	N	%	N	%	N	%	N	%	N	%		
1.	21-30	15	29	19	22	15	14	19	22	9	13.2	8	22.8	6	18.7	17	22.4	108	20.0
2.	31-40	26	56	40	48	42	39	40	48	32	47.1	14	40.6	14	43.6	34	44.8	242	45.0
3.	41-50	5	9.6	21	25	38	35	21	25	24	35.3	9	25.7	8	25	16	21	142	26.3
4.	51-60	4	7.6	4	5	11	10	4	5	3	4.4	4	11.5	4	12.5	5	6.6	39	7.2
5.	61 and above	2	3.8	–	–	2	2	–	–	–	–	–	–	–	–	4	5.2	10	1.0
	Total	52	100	84	100	108	100	84	100	68	100	35	100	32	100	76	100	539	100

Source: Computed.

Of the total respondents, nearly 71 per cent are in the age group of 31 to 50 and 20 per cent in the age group of 21 to 30. It is evident that young and middle aged group women have come to power.

Table 16 : Distribution of Respondents by Educational Qualification

Sl. No.	Category	DGL		TRH		PUD		SIV		RAM		THE		KAR		VIRD		Total	%
		N	%	N	%	N	%	N	%	N	%	N	%	N	%	N	%		
1.	Illiterate	1	2	1	1	2	2	4	5	7	10.2	5	14.3	2	6.2	5	6.6	27	5.0
2.	1-5th Std	0	0	2	2	45	43	2	2	22	32.4	4	11.4	10	31.2	20	26.4	105	19.0
3.	6-8th Std	14	27	26	31	42	41	26	31	19	17.9	11	31.5	5	15.7	18	23.7	166	31.0
4.	9-10th Std	24	46.1	29	35	6	6	30	35	10	14.7	7	20.0	9	28.2	20	26.4	135	25.0
5.	11-12th Std	6	11.5	17	20	6	6	19	23	5	7.4	4	11.4	4	12.5	10	13	71	13.0
6.	Degree / Diploma	7	13.4	9	11	2	2	3	4	5	7.4	4	11.4	2	6.2	3	3.9	35	7.0
	Total	52	100	84	100	108	100	84	100	68	100	35	100	32	100	76	100	539	100

Source: Computed.

Of the respondents 88 per cent have undergone schooling from 1st standard to 12th standard. Only 5 per cent are illiterate while 7 per cent have graduation as their educational background. It is evident that 95 per cent of the respondents are able to read and write which is sufficient to manage the panchayat institutions.

Table 17 : Distribution of Respondents by Religion

Sl. No.	Category	DGL		TRH		PUD		SIV		RAM		THE		KAR		VIRD		Total	%
		N	%	N	%	N	%	N	%	N	%	N	%	N	%	N	%		
1.	Hindu	49	94	81	96	103	95.4	80	95	58	85.3	33	94.3	32	100	71	93.4	507	94
2.	Christian	3	6	3	4	4	3.7	4	5	6	8.8	2	5.7	–	–	4	5.2	26	5
3.	Muslim	–	–	–	–	1	0.9	–	–	4	5.9	–	–	–	–	1	1.4	6	1
	Total	52	100	84	100	108	100	84	100	68	100	35	100	32	100	76	100	539	100

Source: Computed.

Of the respondents 94 per cent are Hindus, 5 per cent are Christians and 1 per cent are Muslims.

Table 18 : Distribution of Respondents by Community

Sl. No.	Category	DGL		TRH		PUD		SIV		RAM		THE		KAR		VIRD		Total	%
		N	%	N	%	N	%	N	%	N	%	N	%	N	%	N	%		
1.	OC	1	2	2	2	1	1	2	2	4	5.9	–	–	–	–	–	–	10	2
2.	BC	36	69.3	50	60	60	56	49	58	33	48.5	17	49	18	56.2	45	60.0	308	57
3.	SC	11	21	17	20	19	18	18	21	24	35.3	8	23	6	18.8	15	20.0	118	22
4.	MBC	4	7.8	12	14	23	21	13	17	6	8.8	10	23	8	25	14	18.2	90	17
5.	ST	–	–	–	–	–	–	2	2	1	1.5	–	–	–	–	2	1.6	5	1
6.	Didn't say	–	–	3	4	5	4	–	–	–	–	–	–	–	–	–	–	8	1
	Total	52	100	84	100	108	100	84	100	68	100	35	100	32	100	76	100	539	100

Source: Computed.

Of the respondents, 22 per cent are from SC, 57 per cent from BC and 17 per cent from MBC. Nearly 96 per cent of the respondents belong to BC, MBC and SC categories. It is clear that power has gone downwards much beyond expectation.

Table 19 : Distribution of Respondents by Occupation

Sl. No.	Category	DGL		TRH		PUD		SIV		RAM		THE		KAR		VIRD		Total	%
		N	%	N	%	N	%	N	%	N	%	N	%	N	%	N	%		
1.	Non-Agriculture	3	6	19	23	6	6	10	12	2	2.9	3	9	–	–	53	70.0	96	19
2.	Agriculture	46	88	65	77	102	94	60	71	63	92.7	29	82	29	90.7	6	8	400	72
3.	Business	–	–	–	–	–	–	5	6	2	2.9	3	9	2	6.2	9	12	21	4
4.	Private Employee	–	–	–	–	–	–	5	6	–	–	–	–	–	–	5	6	10	2
5.	Government Staff	–	–	–	–	–	–	4	5	1	1.5	–	–	1	3.1	3	4	9	2
6.	Didn't say	3	6	–	–	–	–	–	–	–	–	–	–	–	–	–	–	3	1
	Total	52	100	84	100	108	100	84	100	68	100	35	100	32	100	76	100	539	100

Source: Computed.

Here it is to be noted that occupation refers to the occupation of the males of the respondents' families. 72 per cent of the respondents belong to agricultural families and 19 per cent are agricultural coolies. It is seen that both male and female panchayati leaders have the same background either agriculture or agricultural coolie.

Table 20 : Distribution of Respondents by Landholdings

No	Category	DGL		TRH		PUD		SIV		RAM		THE		KAR		VIRD		Total	%
		N	%	N	%	N	%	N	%	N	%	N	%	N	%	N	%		
1.	Landless	8	15	5	6	5	4	9	11	24	35.3	8	22.8	6	18.7	23	30.2	88	17
2.	Marginal Farmers (1 to 5 acres)	15	29	49	58	84	78	49	58	40	58.8	14	40.0	14	43.8	38	50	303	56
3.	Small Farmers (6 to 10 acres)	11	21	7	8	6	6	14	17	4	5.9	8	22.8	8	25	7	9.2	65	12
4.	Big Farmers (more than 11 acres)	11	21	5	6	4	4	7	8	–	–	5	14.4	4	12.5	8	10.6	44	8
5.	Didn't say	7	14	18	22	9	8	5	6	–	–	–	–	–	–	–	–	39	7
	Total	52	100	84	100	108	100	84	100	68	100	35	100	32	100	76	100	539	100

Source: Computed.

This is yet another area where the status of the husband or any male in the family is reflected. 76 per cent of the respondents have landholdings ranging from one acre to 12 acres. (These lands are in the names of their husbands or any other male of the family) while 17 per cent belong to the landless category.

Table 21 : Distribution of Respondents by Annual Income

Sl. No.	Category	DGL		TRH		PUD		SIV		RAM		THE		KAR		VIRD		Total	%
		N	%	N	%	N	%	N	%	N	%	N	%	N	%	N	%		
1.	Less than Rs.10,000	15	29	23	27.3	41	38	15	18	29	44.7	5	14.3	8	2.5	20	26.4	156	29
2.	Rs.10,001 to Rs.20,000	10	19	39	46.4	46	43	39	46	26	38.2	8	22.8	17	53.1	30	39.5	215	39
3.	Rs.20,001 and Rs.30,000	16	31	6	7.2	7	6	16	19	11	16.2	10	28.6	3	9.3	10	13.1	79	15
4.	Rs.30,001 and above	8	15	10	12	3	3	9	11	2	2.9	12	34.3	4	12.6	16	21	64	12
5.	Didn't say	3	6	6	7.1	11	10	5	6	–	–	–	–	–	–	–	–	25	5
	Total	52	100	84	100	108	100	84	100	68	100	35	100	32	100	76	100	539	100

Source: Computed.

Of the respondents, 83 per cent have an income range of Rs.1000 to Rs.30000. Only 12 per cent of the respondents have income above Rs.30,000.

Table 22 : Distribution of Respondents by type of Family

Sl. No.	Category	DGL		TRH		PUD		SIV		RAM		THE		KAR		VIRD		Total	%
		N	%	N	%	N	%	N	%	N	%	N	%	N	%	N	%		
1.	Joint Family	20	38	33	39	35	32	30	36	21	30.4	10	28.6	12	37.5	30	39.5	191	35
2.	Nuclear Family	32	62	51	61	73	68	54	64	47	69.1	25	71.4	20	62.5	46	60.5	348	65
	Total	52	100	84	100	108	100	84	100	68	100	35	100	32	100	76	100	539	100

Source: Computed.

Of the respondents, 65 per cent are in nuclear families and 35 per cent are living in the joint family system.

Table 23 : Details of House Owned by Respondents

Sl. No.	Category	DGL		TRH		PUD		SIV		RAM		THE		KAR		VIRD		Total	%
		N	%	N	%	N	%	N	%	N	%	N	%	N	%	N	%		
1.	Own House	32	62	77	91	107	99	76	90	55	80.9	35	100	30	94	66	86.9	478	88
2.	Rent	20	38	4	5	1	1	8	10	13	19.1	–	–	2	6	10	13.1	58	11
3.	Didn't say	–	–	3	4	–	–	–	–	–	–	–	–	–	–	–	–	3	1
	Total	52	100	84	100	108	100	84	100	68	100	35	100	32	100	76	100	539	100

Source: Computed.

Of the respondents 88 per cent own a house and the others live in rented houses.

Table 24 : Type of House

Sl. No.	Category	DGL		TRH		PUD		SIV		RAM		THE		KAR		VIRD		Total	%
		N	%	N	%	N	%	N	%	N	%	N	%	N	%	N	%		
1.	Hut	7	13	–	–	61	57	21	25	7	10.3	6	13.2	1	3.1	6	7.9	109	24
2.	Tiled	23	44	–	–	12	11	27	32	49	72.1	7	20	19	59.4	22	29	159	35
3.	Pucca	15	29	–	–	22	20	33	39	10	14.7	20	57	11	34.4	44	57.8	155	34
4.	IAY Group House	4	8	–	–	7	6	3	4	2	2.9	2	5	1	3.1	4	5.3	23	5
5.	Didn't say	3	6	–	–	6	6	–	–	–	–	–	–	–	–	–	–	9	2
	Total	52	100	84	100	108	100	84	100	68	100	35	100	32	100	76	100	539	100

Source: Computed.

Of the respondents, 24 per cent live in huts, 35 per cent in tiled houses and only 34 per cent in *pucca* houses. While 5 per cent of the respondents got houses only under Government schemes.

Table 25 : Distribution of Household facilities of the Respondents

Sl. No	Category	DGL				TRY				PUD				SIV				RAM				THE				KAR				VIRD				TOTAL			
		Yes	%	No	%	Yes	%	No	%	Yes	%	No	%	Yes	%	No	%	Yes	%	No	%	Yes	%	No	%	Yes	%	No	%	Yes	%	No	%	Yes	%	No	%
1.	Electricity	47	90	5	10	82	98	2	2	102	94	6	6	80	95	4	5	59	86.8	9	13.2	29	82.9	6	17.1	32	100	-	-	72	94.7	4	5.3	503	93.3	36	6.7
2.	Toilet	34	65	18	35	53	63	31	37	49	45	59	55	54	64	30	36	42	61.8	26	38.2	20	57.1	15	42.9	23	71.8	9	28.2	49	64.4	27	35.6	324	60.1	215	39.9
3.	Water Connection	29	56	23	44	63	75	21	45	31	39	77	71	65	77	19	23	20	229.4	48	70.6	21	60	14	40	11	34.3	21	65.7	32	42.2	42	55.3	272	50.5	267	49.5

Source: Computed.

Of the participants 93.3 per cent, 60.1 per cent and 50 per cent are having electricity, toilet and drinking water facilities respectively in their houses.

Table 26 : Political Party Affiliation of the Respondents

Sl. No.	Category	DGL		TRH		PUD		SIV		RAM		THE		KAR		VIRD		Total	%
		N	%	N	%	N	%	N	%	N	%	N	%	N	%	N	%		
1.	AIADMK	08	15.4	23	27.4	21	19.5	30	35.7	14	20.5	16	45.7	10	31.2	10	13.1	132	24.6
2.	DMK	06	11.5	19	22.6	12	11.2	16	19.0	5	7.4	4	11.4	1	3.1	4	5.7	67	12.5
3.	Congress	03	5.8	05	6.0	0.8	7.5	0.5	5.9	4	5.8	2	5.7	2	6.2	2	2.6	31	5.7
4.	MDMK	03	5.8	02	2.4	03	2.7	10	11.9	–	–	3	8.6	1	3.1	–	–	22	4.0
5.	BJP	01	1.9	01	1.2	02	1.8	04	4.7	–	–	–	–	–	–	4	2.6	12	2.1
6.	Communist	02	3.8	02	2.4	06	5.6	03	3.5	2	2.9	–	–	–	–	–	–	15	2.7
7.	Unanimous	29	55.8	32	38.1	56	51.8	16	19.0	43	63.4	10	28.6	18	56.3	56	73.6	260	48.2
	Total	52	100	84	100	108	100	84	100	68	100	35	100	32	100	76	100	539	100

Source: Computed.

Among the women representatives, 48.2 per cent do not have any affiliation with any political party. Others have links with political parties for which males in their family are responsible.

Table 27 : Type of Newspaper Reading

Sl. No.	Category	DGL		TRH		PUD		SIV		RAM		THE		KAR		VIRD		Total	%
		N	%	N	%	N	%	N	%	N	%	N	%	N	%	N	%		
1.	Dinamalar	29	24.8	69	19.87	78	19.6	53	22.1	42	20.19	31	24.03	22	18.48	54	24.7	378	21.3
2.	Dinathanthi	24	20.5	62	17.7	67	16.9	51	21.2	39	18.7	28	21.7	19	15.9	49	28.4	339	19.0
3.	Dinamani	15	12.8	27	7.7	39	9.8	27	11.2	18	8.6	12	9.3	12	10.1	31	14.2	181	10.2
4.	Dhinakaran	14	11.9	58	16.6	52	13.1	21	8.7	27	12.9	19	14.7	14	11.9	28	12.7	233	13.2
5.	Dhinaboomi	05	4.3	31	8.9	28	7.1	18	7.5	16	7.7	14	10.9	13	10.9	12	5.0	137	7.8
6.	Kalaikathir	04	3.4	39	11.2	34	8.6	12	4.9	11	5.3	8	6.2	11	9.2	05	2.3	124	6.9
7.	Theekathir	05	4.3	18	5.2	23	5.8	09	3.7	13	6.2	5	3.9	6	5.1	11	5	90	5
8.	Namathu MGR	06	5.13	42	12.0	49	12.4	25	10.4	32	15.4	12	9.3	18	15.1	18	8.2	202	11.4
9.	Non Readers	15	12.8	3	0.9	27	6.8	24	9.9	10	4.8	–	–	4	3.3	10	4.5	93	5.2
	Total	117	–	349	–	397	–	240	–	208	–	129	–	119	–	218	–	1777	100

Of the respondents nearly 70 per cent are regular readers of newspapers. It is a welcome sign. The rest of them also read newspapers but not on a regular basis.

Problems Faced by the Panchayat Leaders (Men)

1. Organizing people and making them involve themselves in the developmental activities and Gram Sabha meetings.
2. Accounting system and auditing procedures.
3. Removal of encroachments. Availing of support and help from the revenue department.
4. Maintenance of records and registers.
5. Absence of meaningful linkages with the sectoral departments.
6. MLA/MP area development fund is spent not on the local felt needs/Gram Sabha priorities.
7. Misguidance by officials/trapped into mistakes.
8. No space for innovations/no encouragement from officials.
9. Inadequacy of grant from the Government.
10. Lack of perception among field officials of the concept of Panchayati Raj System.
11. Lack of clear instruction/guidance in approval of layout/building plan.
12. Block level officials show disparity on party line when dealing with the Gram Panchayats.
13. Lack of control over exploitation of natural resources by vested interests.
14. Lack of coordination in executing welfare activities. Amount is spent but the demands of the people are yet to be fulfilled.
15. Implementation of EAS works — issues in the procurement and distribution of rice to the employees engaged in the activities.
16. PRI activities are not people centred but bureaucracy centred.
17. Lack of gender sensitization in developmental process.
18. Non-availability of Government Orders (GOs).

Problems Faced by Panchayati Leaders (Women)

1. Elected women representatives face isolation when they take steps to remove encroachments on Panchayat

properties and common properties. Women leaders are isolated when they take action against anti-social elements.

2. Sectoral departments and police do not cooperate with women Panchayat Presidents in dealing with issues like liquor and eve teasing even if they are reported.
3. Since women Panchayat Presidents are political, they are not able to get the support of MLAs and MPs or their funds.
4. Domination of officials is in practice and bribery is a common feature.
5. If Vice-Presidents are men, they do not cooperate with the women Presidents.
6. The women Presidents face a lot of problems from their male Vice-Presidents.
7. Vice-Presidents/Panchayat clerks misuse their powers/ positions and as Presidents the women cannot take action against them because they are men.
8. There is a problem in collecting taxes from industries and households. They do not cooperate with the Panchayats.
9. Lack of cooperation from officials/non-officials.
10. Many Presidents are threatened with Section 205 of the Tamil Nadu Panchayat Act of 1994.
11. The major problem is sand quarrying/dyeing units against which government officials do not take any action.
12. With regard to common property resources and removal of encroachments there is no cooperation between the Presidents and the block officials.
13. All rural development schemes must be implemented through Panchayats.
14. Basic needs of people cannot be fulfilled. Hence they do not cooperate in Panchayat activities.
15. Women representatives elected to grassroots level institutions have been facing numerous problems within their families, in their social, political and administrative settings. This has often led to ineffective administration of these bodies by the women leaders.

Questions Raised by Trainees (Men)

In the capacity building exercise, after the delivery of key details as per the schedule, the participants were asked to share their doubts or seek clarifications if any on the subject dealt with by the resource persons. Such question and answer sessions were very lively. It provided opportunity to each participant. The following were the areas on which the participants raised questions.

1. How can we stop the illegal mining of sand in the area of the Panchayat?
2. How can we rectify the audit objections in Panchayat administration?
3. Who is the competent authority to finalise the BPL list?
4. How can we sensitise the people on social development?
5. What is the basic difference between executive authority and President?
6. What is the procedure to dismiss the Panchayat clerk if he commits mistakes?
7. Can the Panchayat construct houses in *natham poramboke* for SC and ST people?
8. What is social audit?
9. Is it mandatory that the Panchayat formulate 7 committees?
10. How can we bring about coordination among the sectoral departments?
11. How is house tax revised and how are we to handle this issue?
12. Are there any options to augment income without enhancing the house tax?
13. Is any scheme available to undertake tree planting activities on a sustainable basis? Whom have we to contact in this regard?
14. Can we convene the Panchayat meeting during holidays?
15. Can we convene the Gram Sabha in spite of the non-availability of the nodal officer?
16. Will it be possible for the President to keep an identity card?

17. If for any activity, the Gram panchayat administration spends additionally over and above the allocation, how can we get reimbursement of the same?
18. What are the different kinds of Panchayat meetings and what is the quorum for each?
19. Can we levy a tax on the advertisement related to the election campaign?
20. To create employment opportunities what activities have Panchayat Presidents to undertake?
21. What is the procedure for the appointment of local engineers for Panchayat civil works?
22. What is the procedure for permitting temporary shops on the roadside?
23. When any government programmes are organised at village level, the name of MLA/MP is printed in the invitation whereas the name of the Gram President is being ignored. How can we handle this?
24. What is the procedure for fixing professional tax?
25. For more than 7 years one individual has failed to pay the house tax. What action has the Panchayat to take against him?
26. To whom is insurance coverage applicable among the Panchayat staff?
27. SFC grant deduction is made without the knowledge of the Panchayats. How can this be handled?
28. SHGs are deal directly with officials only and not with the Panchayats. How can this be handled?
29. The official communication submitted to the District Collector by the Panchayat get no response. What can the Panchayat do about this?
30. The ward members do not show interest in Panchayat meetings. They do not attend. How can we could tackle this?
31. A resource centre is needed at the Union level to clarify the day-to-day issues. We cannot expect that all the steps will be taught by the officials. How can a resource institution be established in each block?
32. The mindset of the bureaucrats is not for decenralisation. How can we reset the same?

33. Can we purchase a TV set? What procedure have we to follow?
34. What is the procedure for allotting *poramboke*?
35. What is the procedure for auctioning trees and ponds to augment income?
36. What procedures have we to follow to erect a cycle stand in highways land?
37. Organisers of social celebrations/festival celebrations demand donations from Presidents, but without salary how can the President meet all these expenses?
38. Can the Panchayat remove encroachments on *natham poramboke* where cultivation is taking place there?
39. How are we to levy tax on industries and other business houses?
40. Can the Panchayat run ration shops?
41. Why is not salary fixed for Panchayat leaders even though they are discharging many duties and responsibilities?
42. How are we to get details of the properties of the Panchayat?
43. What action can be taken against the Vice-President in the event of his/her refusing to sign the cheque?
44. Can the Panchayat clerk undertake Panchayat works as contractor?
45. Who will help the Panchayat in preparation of planning?
46. How can we mobilize people for the Gram Sabha when people in the villages are divided on caste and political basis?
47. Who will evince interest in the Gram Sabha meeting when the Gram Sabha decisions are not respected by the officials?
48. How are we to remove encroachments on the common properties?
49. What can be done by the Panchayats in the event of non-cooperation of the revenue officials for removal of encroachments?
50. What economic activities can be initiated by the Panchayat?

51. How can the panchayat ensure social justice in the absence of police power to the Panchayat?
52. How can the Panchayat take action against the EB for its negligence?
53. How are we to change the attitude of the officials towards the Panchayat?
54. Can the Panchayat run a cable TV to increase the income of the Panchayat?
55. How are we to remove bogus ration cards?
56. How are we to identify the families actually living below the poverty line?
57. How are we to control the illicit arrack mafia in the rural areas?
58. How are we to settle the disputes between the officials of the PWD and the Department of Forests in determining the harvest of the trees in the tanks?
59. Can we impose a tax on the buildings/hostels of private engineering colleges in the rural areas?
60. How are we to take action against defaulters of professional tax and house tax?
61. What can be done when the layouts have been wrongly approved by the former Gram Panchayat President?
62. What can be done when the former Panchayat President has not handed over records and charge to the present incumbent?
63. Can a Panchayat leader apply for leave for 3 months?
64. Whom has the Panchayat approach for getting *patta* for the poor?
65. How are we to select IAY beneficiaries?
66. How are we to establish linkage with SHGs in the Panchayat area?
67. What are we to do when houses have been constructed without the approval of the Panchayat?
68. How are we to take action against erring Panchayat clerks?
69. Who is responsible for the Panchayat records? Clerk/President?
70. Can the Panchayat remove 2C *Patta*?

71. How are we to change the mindset of the people who expect everything from the Panchayat?
72. Can we get training continuously?
73. Will you organise a refresher programme?
74. Why do sectoral departments not inform the Panchayats about their activities in the Panchayat area?
75. Why are leaders not brought under the Panchayat system?
76. What can be done in the event of the police not cooperating with the Panchayat?
77. Why do District Collectors take action against Panchayat Presidents without adhering to procedures and rules?
78. Why does the Government deduct EB bill at its end instead of asking the Panchayats to remit the money in the EB office?
79. Is it necessary that all the members of the Council sign the resolution book?
80. What is the duty of the nodal officer who attends the Gram Sabha?
81. Who has the power to remove the trees in the Panchayat area?
82. What action can be taken by the President against individuals evade house tax?
83. What action can be taken against individuals who have not paid the water charges?
84. How can we get government orders in Tamil?
85. What can be done when there is no proper taking over and handing over?
86. Can the Panchayat President dismiss the sweeper if his/her performance is not satisfactory?
87. Can the public attend the Panchayat Council meeting as observers?

Questions Raised by Trainees (Women)

Ramnad District

1. How does the Government determine which constituencies are to be reserved for *Dalits*?

2. How are the traditional Panchayat and its constitutional counterpart to be related?
3. Why does the Government not release SFC grants on time?
4. How can Panchayat Presidents approve building plans?
5. What action can we take against the Vice-President if he/she refuses to sign a cheque without giving a reason?
6. Are there any procedures by which Panchayats can exercise control over the location of sanitary complexes?
7. Whom should we approach for information regarding the local area development schemes of MLAs and MPs?
8. What facilities can we use to solve the water problem?
9. How should we take action against those who do not pay the house tax?
10. What is the procedure for buying a new Panchayat television set?
11. Are tanks, ponds, and canals the property of Panchayats or the PWD?
12. Why do Panchayats not get jurisdiction over the MLA's schemes?
13. Why does the *natham poramboke* exist and how should we deal with encroachments on *natham poramboke* lands?
14. What is "surcharge"?
15. How can we avoid audit objections?
16. Can the Panchayat run the ration shop?
17. What should we do when people initiate construction without first obtaining the Panchayat's building approval?
18. Why is the Government not prompt in implementing the Swajaldhara Scheme, despite the fact that the Panchayat is conscientious about making its contribution?
19. How can the Panchayat take steps against the owners of buildings in public places that are hazardous?
20. Can we collect taxes from the owners of private schools, buildings, and banks?
21. Can the Panchayat take loans to fund its activities?
22. What financial institutions provide assistance to rural development activities?

Theni District

1. What are the procedures for conducting meetings?
2. How many people must be there for a Panchayat to fulfil the quorum requirement?
3. What action can be taken against the Vice-President and ward members if they do not cooperate during a Panchayat meeting?
4. Can a disabled individual become President or hold any other position in the Panchayat?
5. How does the State Finance Commission's apportion funds? How should it actually go about devolving these funds to the Panchayats?
6. Should the Panchayat repay the water connection deposit to households that are leaving the village?
7. What action can be taken against the Village Administrative Officer if he/she does not cooperate with the Panchayat?
8. How can one suspend the Vice-President or the Panchayat clerk?
9. If someone is using Panchayat land how should this encroachments be removed?
10. How can a Panchayat take action against the EB for its negligence?
11. Should a President legitimize the landholdings of a person who has encroached on common property with the permission of the previous President?
12. If there is a damaged tree beside the highway should the Panchayat cut it or lease it out?
13. How can we change the attitude of the officials?
14. Can we collect taxes from NGOs and Kalayana Mandabam if they are running hostels for profit?
15. The public refuse to accept an increase in the house tax but the Panchayat needs more funding. How can we change the mindset of the public?
16. How can we take action against the clerk if he commits fraud?

Virudhunagar District

1. Can a Panchayat appoint a Charted Accountant?
2. How is the PDS to be handled effectively?
3. Who is responsible for the delayed disbursement funds to panchayats?
4. How are we to change the mindset of the ward members?
5. How are we to remove encroachment?
6. What action can the Panchayat take against corrupt people?
7. Explain the Government protocols?
8. Explain the means by which the panchayat can improve the condition of SC/ST people?
9. How are we to coordinate the Panchayat activities with SHGs' activities?

Karur District

1. Who is responsible for the maintenance of records, the clerk or the President?
2. The Revenue Department does not cooperate in the removal of encroachments. What can be done?
3. How can we select beneficiaries for Government schemes?
4. How are we to take action against fraudulent Panchayat clerks?
5. How can we mobilize the people for the Gram Sabha?
6. How are we to promote the economic activities in the rural areas?
7. How are we to find out the real below poverty line families?
8. What is 2C *patta*?
9. The people expect each and everything from the Panchayat. How are we to change the mindset?
10. Is suspension of the Village Panchayat President under the section 205 by the District Collector because of holding executive authority correct?

Sivagangai District

1. What action can be taken against the Vice-President if he refuses to cooperate with the President in carrying out the Panchayat activities?
2. What is to be done when the forest department do not pay the dues to the Panchayat?
3. What power is vested with the Panchayat to take action against individuals who refuse to pay professional tax and house tax?
4. Is the Panchayat eligible to get revenue share from leasing and billing of minor minerals? If so how much?
5. Can the Panchayat sue the State government?
6. Can the Panchayat President be sued by any individual?
7. What action can be taken against the construction of buildings without the approval of the Panchayat?

Pre-Training Evaluation (Men)

The Panchayat leaders believe that the Panchayat is only an implementing agency and it should implement schemes and programmes. They believe that basic amenities are the major responsibility of the Panchayats. Meeting the needs of the people is the basis of the Panchayati Raj System. They are not aware of gender justice and social justice and they do not know the accounting procedures. They do not know about Panchayat administration and finance. They are not independent and they are afraid of the officials.

They are aware that women and *Dalit* will also get opportunities to serve in the Panchayati Raj System. But few respondents are aware of the schemes of the Central and State governments. Totally independent activities are not possible at the Panchayat level. They do not know about the 29 subjects. They are not aware of the Tamil Nadu Panchayat Act, 1994 and its provisions. With regard to the functions of the Panchayat, they do not know the obligatory functions and the discretionary functions. Further they are not aware of the government grants and local resources for Panchayat development. They are not aware of the full implications of the Gram Sabhas.

They believe that MLAs/MPs have powers to solve the problems of the people. They feel that Panchayat Presidents have to carry out the works given by the officials. From the training programme they expect a clear explanation for the concept of power. They need information pertinent to Panchayat administration. They demand guidelines from the resource persons to augment resources for Panchayats. They need more details about accounting procedures and audit formalities.

1. *The following are the factors responsible for their success to them in the election :*

- Social service in the villages.
- Free movement with the people.
- Functional efficiency shown in other public activities.
- Socio-economic background.
- Public relations/Public activities.
- Association with SHGs and the youth.
- Self-confidence.
- Village youth.
- NYK coordinators.
- Officials.
- Party members.
- Selvi J. Jayalalitha, Chief Minister of Tamil Nadu.
- Settling public issues.
- Understanding the perception and practice of government officials.
- Improving the relationship among opponents.
- Acquiring knowledge of administration.
- Understanding the formation and functioning of CBOs.
- Understanding the level of poverty.
- Understanding the importance of people's participation.

Most of the respondents could understand the dual role to be performed by the President of the Gram Panchayat.

2. *After being elected Presidents, they are developing their leadership qualities in the following ways :*
    - Relationship with officials, family friends, party members.
    - Association with SHGs/youth.

3. *Perception of New Panchayat Raj System and 73rd Amendment Act :*

    - Number of development programmes are included in the new Panchayat Raj System.
    - Three tier system.
    - State Finance Commission.
    - Grassroots development.
    - People's participation and development.
    - Third government.
    - Need based works are done.
    - Preference should be given to important works.
    - Gram Sabha meetings.
    - Reservation for women.
    - 29 subjects.
    - State Election Commission.

4. *Duties and responsibilities of Gram Panchayat :*

    - Basic facilities are to be completed, i.e., water supply, sanitation, electricity, housing and road.
    - Tax-collection.
    - Link road facility.
    - Light facility in public places/public roads.
    - Sanitary complex for both men and women.

5. *Gram Sabha activities :*

About Gram Sabha, the respondents in general have a positive opinion. They feel that it is a forum to understand the people's needs, to prioritize the needs, to explain the situation of Panchayat and to educate the masses. At the same time, the respondents remark that in spite of sincere efforts initiated for mobilizing the people, the villagers fail to give proper importance to the Gram Sabha. They expect that all the resolutions of the Gram Sabha should be realized. The respondents maintain that people's participation has to be increased. About Gram Sabha, they hold the following views :

- Villagers considered it grievance-day meeting.
- All the resolutions are to be executed without fail.
- Transparency.
- More awareness is essential for strengthening Gram Sabha activities.
- Planning is essential for further development.
- Based on financial resources planning process is to be formulated.
- Various demands are placed in the Gram Sabha meeting.
- Local problems are solved in the Gram Sabha meeting.
- More women members participate.
- Nodal officers do not inform the Gram Sabha any schemes related to Panchayat development.

6. *Participation in Panchayat Development Activities :*

- 70 per cent of the people participate and 30 per cent of the people do not. The respondents say that people's participation is based on their own interests.
- All the villagers believe that the Gram Panchayat should do all the development works.
- Selection of BPL persons is not satisfactory. So they have not participated. They are not getting any benefit from the Gram Panchayat.

7. *Participation in training programme :*

- District level training at Collectorate.
- SIRD, Maraimalainagar, Chennai.
- RECT.
- Gandhigram Rural Institute.
- A few NGOs provide training.

- 50 per cent of the respondents said that Gandhigram Rural Institute organised the first training programme for Presidents.

8. Government Programmes :

The respondents are aware of the following schemes :

- DRDA schemes.
- SGRY & SGSY for self-employment.
- 11th Finance Commission fund.
- Free Cycle to Adi Dravidas.
- MLA/MP Schemes.
- Self-Employment.
- Rajiv Gandhi National Drinking Water Mission Scheme.
- Mahalir Thittam.
- Rainwater harvesting.
- Individual toilets for each house.
- Group houses for weaker sections.
- School toilets.
- Sarva Siksha Abhiyan.
- Small Savings Scheme.
- IAY.
- PMGSY.
- Village self-sufficiency scheme.
- Anna Yojana.
- Area Development.
- Swajaldhara.
- DPAP.

Most of these schemes are implemented through the Rural Development Department. The respondents are not aware of the availability of other schemes of various sectors.

9. Expectations from the training their needs are :

- Panchayat Act rules/regulations.
- Guidance for efficient administration.

- Guidance for making their Panchayat a model.
- Duties/responsibilities/powers of Panchayat Presidents.
- Financial details/fund allocation system.
- Panchayat Raj System in nearby States like Kerala, Karnataka and Andhra Pradesh.
- How to develop the SC community?
- Meetings and procedures.
- Building approval procedure.
- Layout approval procedure.
- NGO orientation.
- SFC details.
- Details of decentralization of power in respect of the 29 subjects.
- District level training centre.
- Extension of training programmes.
- Detailed knowledge of development schemes.
- Details of schemes for the SC community.
- Regular tax collection methods.
- Auction sources.
- Stamp duty details.
- Avoiding recovery from SFC grant.
- Accounting/Audit procedure.
- Periodical training.
- Follow-up training.

They ask for the training in the following areas :

- Management of Gram Panchayat.
- Management of common properties.
- Panchayat Finance.
- Organizing Gram Sabha.
- Panchayats in social development.
- Women/*Dalit* empowerment.
- Powers of the Panchayat President.
- Powers of the Gram Panchayat.
- Section 205 of the Tamil Nadu Panchayat Act.

Post-Training Evaluation (Men)

After attending the training programmes, majority of the Gram Panchayat Presidents have established a grip over the bases of decentralization and its implications for the society. They are aware of the basic principles of the 73rd Amendment to the Constitution of India. They have gained knowledge of the following :

- Supply driven to demand driven activities.
- Working for economic development of rural areas.
- Administering social development.
- Working for the poor and the marginalized.
- Planning at the grassroots.
- Mobilizing resources from within.
- Working for achieving 100 per cent literacy.
- Working for reducing school dropout rate.
- Working for reducing infant mortality rate.
- Protecting the well-being of women and children.
- Retrieving children from malnutrition.
- Making the village resourceful.
- Extending all necessary assistance expected by village community.
- Ensuring development of each family.
- Devolution of finance directly to the people.
- Administering social justice.
- Protecting/promoting common property resources in villages.
- Gaining correct perspective.
- Priorities.
- Bases of decentralization of powers.
- Audit and accounting procedures.
- Social justice and gender justice.
- Importance of participation of people in development.
- Leadership quality.
- Managing common property resources.
- Schemes and programmes for rural development.
- Importance of SHGs.
- Micro-level planning.

— Women's empowerment.
— Water supply and sanitation.
— Micro enterprises/micro finance.
— Environment development.
— 73rd Constitutional Amendment Act.
— Three-tier system.
— Panchayat administration.
— Sources of income and economic development.
— Tax collection.
— Basic facilities.
— Building plan approval/layout approval.
— Auction procedures.
— Relationship with officials/non-officials.
— Preparing annual plan.
— Transparency in administration.

1. *Objectives of the New Panchayat Raj System*

- To establish sub-reliant administration.
- To fulfil the felt needs of the people.
- To immediately attend to the people's issues.
- To carry out schemes properly.
- To realize the dream of Gandhiji in "Gram Swaraj".
- To bring about social justice and economic development.
- Activities for planned socio-economic development.
- Financial sources directly to the people.
- Self-government.
- Benefits for grassroots people.
- Third government for sustainable development.
- Decentralization in 29 subjects.
- To ensure development of each village.
- Three-tier system.
- Power to the people.
- Planning at grassroots level based on demands.

2. *What does Decentralization mean?*

- It is a first government.
- Transfer of power from government to people.

- Formation of third tier of government nearer to the people.
- To coordinate with the all sectoral departments.
- To establish governance at the local level.
- To involve all concerned in governance.
- To recognize local initiatives.
- Meant for people's participation.
- Planning from below/power to the people.
- Delivery of services to the people.

3. *Impact of Decentralization*

- Delay is avoided.
- Poorest among the poor are targeted.
- Self-sufficiency and self-reliance are realized.
- Sensitizing to one's own responsibilities.
- Transparency and honesty in administration.
- People's participation in governance.
- More resources are augmented for rural development.
- Democracy is getting strengthened.
- Availing of all assistance properly.
- Fund utility reaches the needy.
- Power is empowering people.
- Panchayati Raj Institutions become a permanent entity.
- Village development is projected and each village has to be benefited.
- Responsibilities are shared among the elected representatives as well as the community.
- Wasteful activities/expenditures are avoided.
- Enormous scope for self-sustenance.
- Helps to run the Panchayat efficiently.

4. *Duties/Responsibilities of Gram Panchayat*

- Providing basic facilities to people/schemes/programmes.
- Planned financial transaction.
- Creation of infrastructure facilities.
- To establish social justice.

- To ensure environment cleanliness.
- Initiating plan for development.
- To disseminate the details of schemes/programmes of government to the people.
- Convening of Panchayat/Gram Sabha meeting.
- Preparation of agenda and communication to all concerned.
- Giving priority to the people.
- Provision of quality education.
- Monitoring the functioning of PDS.
- Promotion of environmental sanitation.
- Obligatory and discretionary functions.
- Giving priority to the people.

5. *Ways/means to augment financial sources*

- By enhancing the taxes.
- By collecting the taxes fully as per the demand.
- Sales proceedings from compost manure.
- Avail all eligible grants.
- Improve the CPR activities.
- Resource mobilization through CPR.
- Ensure people's contribution.
- Maintain relationship with concerned officials / departments.

It is learnt that, the Gram Panchayat Presidents properly realize that the major sources of income are tax collection and utilization of CPR.

6. *Procedures to be adopted in Planning*

- Draft in the Panchayat and get approval from Gram Sabha.
- It should favour the felt needs/priorities.
- Comprehensive plan after calculating the factors like fund availability, population, Panchayat fund and scope for people's contribution.

- Plan for infrastructure development also.
- Ensure benefit of plan to all/ensure joint responsibilities.
- Adopt scientific approach.
- Explain time management to people.
- Make use of SHGs.
- Based on Gram Sabha decision planning process goes on.
- Annual plan/five year plan is formulated.
- Women involved in the planning process.
- Consult block officials and ex-Panchayat President.
- Plan according to the availability of funds.

7. *Procedure to be followed in the maintenance of accounts*

- Collect all the procedures regarding the 31 registers.
- Regular passbook and cashbook verification.
- Entries should be made everyday in all registers.
- Clear cut transaction in all four accounts.
- Explaining the system to the Vice-President/Ward Members.
- List the sources of income/expenditure.
- Properly refer to rules/regulations in this regard.
- Keep all the records in a proper almirah safely.

After the training the respondents have realized that they are held responsible for the accounts. Earlier it was said that they depended on the clerk.

8. *To Effect Social Development*

- Proper linkage between State Government and Panchayati Raj Institutions.
- Proper attention to the welfare of women/children.
- Special attention to destitutes, orphans, poor widows.
- Equitable services to *Dalit* community.
- Associate with NGOs/youth.
- Sanitation for all.
- Plan for the development of the youth.

- Abolition of child labour.
- Emphasis on primary education/health.
- Promote animal husbandry activities.
- Library facilities.
- Encourage people's participation in Gram Sabha meeting.
- Ensure protected roof to all houses.
- Ensure the provision of public toilets and their proper utilisation.
- Avail the assistance and guidance of NGOs, SHGs and CBOs in social development activities.
- Communication skills.
- Ensure participation of people.
- Humanness.
- Accountability to the public.
- Understand government systems and procedures.
- Loans to be issued to the needy persons.
- Protection of village environment.

9. *Qualities required for Leadership*

- Self-confidence and boldness.
- Desilting works at the local level.
- Information, education and knowledge on the concept and functioning of Panchayat Raj System.
- Service mind, honesty and character.
- Respect the people and involve them.
- Fair deal.
- Treat all equally.
- Adherence to rules/procedures.
- Properly and humbly explain the issues to the people.
- Accountability.
- Patience and regard when dealing with the public/officials.
- Controlling and regulating power.
- Decentralization in task assignment.
- Vision clarity.

- Sensitization in social justice.
- Emotional balance.
- Not agitated over people's demand and pressure.
- Good rapport with officials and Ward Members.
- Mentality to treat enemies as friends.
- Gender sensitization.
- Faith in non-violence.
- Always speak only the truth.
- Avoid unnecessary talk with officials/non-officials.
- Guidance/counselling for local people.
- Panchayat works have to be carried out based on the demands.
- Continuous involvement in social welfare activities.
- Decision-making is necessary in development activities.

The above said factors are essential for developing leadership qualities at the Gram Panchayat level.

10. *Approach to Economic Development*

- Sensitizing people to work hard and make efforts.
- Improve the resources of Panchayati Raj Institutions.
- Adopting modern technologies in irrigation activities.
- Promote animal husbandry activities.
- Involve development experts and economists to equip the villagers.
- Collection of taxes/other revenues.
- Instead of privatization encourage nationalization.
- Guide to go for self-employment.
- Appropriate industrial policy.
- Awareness/capacity building for the youth.
- Association with NGOs.
- Ensure participation of people.
- Use water and energy economically.
- Introduce appropriate small scale industries/village industries in rural areas.
- Guidance to farmers.
- Agricultural production.

It was obvious that in the course of the training, the respondents acquired the necessary knowledge of the concept of economic development.

11. *Dalit Development*

- Proper dispensation of government schemes.
- Effective functioning of THADCO.
- Strict adherence to legislations against untouchability.
- Deal fairly and humanely.
- Higher education to the youth.
- Capacity building.
- Proper delivery of assistance to *Dalits,* elimination of child labour and social awareness among *Dalit* community all needed at present.

With regard to development of *Dalits* they preferred employment opportunities and in that more reservation for *Dalits* is needed. They prefer gender sensitization and prevention of untouchability.

12. *Women Development*

- Health Activities.
- Economic/enterprising activities.
- Gender sensitization.
- Compulsory education.
- Women's association.
- Effective functioning of SHGs.
- Pre-natal/Post-natal care.
- Child welfare/child rights.
- 33 per cent of reservation in employment in all departments.
- Proper implementation of RCH, marketing of SHG products, functioning of women sanitary complex etc., will directly have impact on the development of women.

Women's development is properly perceived by the respondents. They understand the strength of SHGs. They emphasize the concept of gender equality and suggest awareness building and education for all women.

13. *What do they need? After the training, they propose to give priority to*

- All government orders.
- Periodical training and sensitization.
- Periodical review of their works.
- Periodical meeting with District Collector and other officials.
- Exposure visit to other good Panchayats.
- Habit of rainwater harvesting.
- Social development activities.
- Becoming a model.
- Making the village a model one.
- Effectively performing the dual role President/executive.
- 100 per cent tax collection.
- SHG activities.

Pre-Training Evaluation (Women)

A total of 539 Gram Panchayat women leaders participated in the training programme. Of them 62 per cent had been elected for the first time. So they were not aware of Panchayat activities. The women leaders contested in the election and won with the support of their family and community. When they contested in the election, they were not aware of anything about the Panchayats. Only after assuming charge and contacting the officials did they come to know that Panchayat leaders have to carry out certain activities in the Panchayats. They were not even aware of the major provisions of the 1994 Tamil Nadu Panchayats Act. By making use of this opportunity, they have developed leadership qualities and established contact with the officials. Their shyness and inhibitions have disappeared. Accordingly they showed awareness of many government schemes and stated that they had received this information from government officers. The majority of them did not know the meaning of the concept of decentralization. They thought that the new Panchayat Raj System is meant to implement the schemes and programmes of the Central and State Governments. Event though they knew a few provisions, they were not aware of the full implications of the Panchayati Raj Act of 1994.

When they were inquired about who motivated them to contest in the election, more than 50 per cent of the Presidents said that it was their husbands, family members or relatives and a very few only said that it was the people. More than 40 per cent of the Presidents said that they had been acting as proxies till then. Some mentioned NGOs while some said that they contested in the election out of their own interest. Some referred to motivation by the local MLAs because of their popularity in the village and their association with political parties.

When they were asked about what factors contributed to their success in the election divergent views emerged and some of them are listed below :

- The confidence reposed in them by the people.
- Familiarity in the village because of their involvement in public activity by performing social work.
- Educational background.
- Social and political involvement of the family members.
- People believed that she was the right person to fulfil their desires and dreams to make their village a model one.
- Village and family members' support.
- Their strong will-power and their desire to perform in public.
- Their honesty and confidence in themselves.
- Involvement in grievance redressal of the people.
- They were honest and led a disciplined life.
- Public cooperation, their approach to the public, personal character.
- Fulfilling the basic needs of the people.

Making use of this opportunity they had developed their personality and acquired the following new traits :

- Leadership quality.
- Realizing the roles and responsibilities of the President.
- Respecting the village people, treating all equally, being kind to people.
- Confidence, perseverance and endurance.
- Serving the poverty stricken people and helping them to lead a decent human life.
- Functioning on the principle of consensus and inculcating the spirit of tolerance.
- Functioning without any bias and working for the welfare of all sections of society.
- Qualities which are very much required to continue in social life.
- Functioning as an agent between the government and the people.
- Administrative capacity.
- Bringing about justice for suppressed women and concentrating on their upliftment.
- Readiness to take on any contingency.

Next their idea about the new Panchayat Raj System was enquired into and many were not able to spell out the basic structure of the new Panchayat Raj System. Their answers were varied :

- To fulfil the basic needs of the people since the Central and the State Governments could not do it.
- For safeguarding common property resources.
- To implement Government schemes through the Gram Sabha.
- Three-tier system of local government.
- List of 29 subjects in the Eleventh Schedule.
- Ensuring social justice and economic equality.
- Reservation for SC/ST people.
- Reservation for women.
- Importance of women's participation in political life.
- Power devolution to make Panchayats as self-governing institutions.

- Tamil Nadu Panchayats Act, 1994.
- State Election Commission.

The next question asked was about the 73rd Amendment. About 40 per cent women Panchayat Presidents were aware of the features of the 73rd Amendment Act. The other didn't know them and they were attending the training programme to learn them. A few clearly mentioned some of the basic features as :

- Gram Sabha.
- Reservation for women and *Dalits*.
- Election every five years.
- Three-tier system.
- Self-governing institutions.
- Devolution of powers on 29 subjects (11th Schedule).
- Planning at grassroots, planning by the people in the Gram Sabha for the village.

The next question was about the roles and functions of the Gram Panchayat Presidents according to the Local Government Act of Tamil Nadu. Of the total participants, very few spelt out their roles and functions and they were :

- To provide basic amenities like safe drinking water, roads, streetlights, health and sanitation.
- Construction of public toilets for women and sensitizing people towards constructing individual toilets.
- The main function of the Gram Sabha is to decide the basic facilities for the Panchayat with the participation of the people.
- Creating consensus among the people to enable the President of Panchayats and the members to pass resolutions is the function of the Gram Sabha.
- The Gram Sabha is a forum to share individual opinion among others.
- The Gram Sabha is a forum to create awareness among people about social issues.

- The Gram Sabha is convened to inform the people about the income and expenditure of the Panchayat.
- To convene and to chair Panchayat meetings every month and to convene Gram Sabha meeting for four times in a year.
- To collect taxes properly, to regulate and to monitor the functioning of the PDS, to plan for the Panchayat (long term and short term plan).
- To maintain and properly utilize common property resources.
- To implement the projects and schemes of State and Central Governments.
- The main function of the Gram Sabha is to select the beneficiaries for government schemes.
- The Gram Sabha has to pass resolutions on various demands of the people.
- There is a mandatory quorum for the Gram Sabha meeting.
- Participation of SHGs in the Gram Sabha is important.
- The Gram Sabha is convened to share divergent views and to work for consensus.
- The Gram Sabha takes care of Social audit, preparing annual plan.
- The Gram Sabha meets to inform people about various government schemes and plans.
- The Gram Sabha gives a good opportunity to the backward and weaker sections and women to voice problems and take decisions.

The next question asked was about the people's participation in the Gram Panchayat. Most of the women Presidents were satisfied with the people's participation in the activities of the Gram Panchayat. Some were very much concerned about the disturbance in the Gram Sabha. Because people are very enthusiastically and eagerly participating in Gram Sabha meetings people say that all rural development schemes must be implemented through Panchayats. People are coming forward to put forth their requirements in the general meeting and particularly, women are more articulate in expressing their needs. The Panchayat Presidents are very much concerned about embarrassing situations like some of the resolutions passed in the meeting not being implemented due to lack of cooperation from the officials. Due to financial constraints the Presidents couldn't fulfil their demands.

People used to ask the Presidents about the action taken on the resolutions passed in the earlier Gram Sabha meeting. But the Presidents couldn't fulfil their demands. In spite of all this, people are cooperating with the Panchayats fully. This shows that cooperation from the government is required to fulfil their dreams.

As for their attendance at previous training programmes only 20 per cent of the women Panchayat Presidents had attended training programmes conducted by various government departments and Gandhigram Rural Institute. The remaining were new to the training programme.

Next they were asked about the various schemes offered by the State and Central Governments. All the participants answered this question and mentioned a few schemes as given below :

1. SGRY and SJRY
2. *Swajaldhara*
3. IAY
4. TRSP
5. Rainwater harvesting
6. Indira Awas Yojana
7. Sarva Siksha Abhiyan
8. PMGSY
9. TANWA
10. Schemes related to disabled
11. Rural Sanitation Programme
12. Namakku Naame Thittam
13. *Chulah*
14. Women and Children Sanitary Complex Scheme
15. MLA and MP constituency fund
16. Anna Marumalarchi Thittam
17. Housing facilities
18. Drinking water scheme

Post-Training Evaluation (Women)

With the help of resource persons and specialists the utility of the training programme was assessed through a questionnaire which was administered at the end of the training programme. The women Panchayat Presidents reported the following:

The first question was about the objectives of the Panchayat Raj System. The responses of the women Panchayat Presidents are given below :

- To provide the basic amenities in the village.
- To plan for the welfare of the people in the Gram Sabha with the help of the people.
- To create a village based on the vision of the late Prime Minister Rajiv Gandhi.
- To ensure the participation of women and weaker sections of the society in governance.
- To make sure to take the government schemes to the needy.
- To create a just society with economic equity.
- To create awareness about common property resources and to maintain the same.
- To provide good governance in grassroots democracy.
- To create awareness about education and provide education to all.
- To empower the people to prioritize their own needs.
- To ensure the development of each family.
- To devolve powers and finances directly to the people.
- To develop the village socially and economically.
- To attain self-sufficiency and to be self-reliant.
- To conduct election for grassroots governance without any lapse.

A few respondents noted that the financial position in the Panchayati Raj Institutions is very bad because the disbursement of funds is delayed. They also said that political parties tend to interfere in the New Panchayat Raj System.

The second question was about "what is meant by the term 'decentralization'?" The responses of the women Panchayat leaders were :

- Constituting State Election Commission, Finance Commission and Planning Committee.
- Reservation for weaker sections of society such as *Dalits* and women in the Panchayats.
- Power given to weaker sections of society to take decisions on the issues affecting their life.
- Roles and responsibilities relating to governance are relevant to the community as a whole, not to just the elected representatives.
- To plan for those who live below the poverty line.
- Three-tier system.
- Work on 29 subjects.
- Ensuring people's participation through the Gram Sabha.
- To implement Government plans and schemes.
- To mobilize funds on their own to perform their functions.

Despite decentralization of powers inadequate devolution of finance prevents Panchayats from fulfilling the goals of development in such areas as education, drinking water supply, environment protection, women and child welfare and health facilities. A few respondents also stated that they had trouble in mobilizing participation.

The third question concerning the impact of decentralization drew the following responses :

— Panchayats can provide the basic amenities to people.

— Panchayats can alleviate poverty through economic activities.

— Panchayats can solve problems and evolve good solutions to them.

The fourth question was about their roles and responsibilities. After the training, the participants were more conscious of their roles and responsibilities than before. They knew the roles and responsibilities to be discharged by the

Presidents, especially women leaders. They admitted that, even without power and money, the Presidents can play a positive role in transforming the rustic folk. This they felt was the impact of the training. Now they realize their role in propagating the importance of pre-natal and post-natal care, because this is very much required for a healthy society. Awareness about health and sanitation should also be created and this will be the sole responsibility of the Panchayat Presidents to free society from chronic diseases. They can seek assistance from the medical officer and sanitary inspectors. They also know about the importance of SHGs and other social organizations like youth club and they have acquired basic information on how to work with them and use them for developmental activities. The other functions and responsibilities that they indicated were :

- Providing basic amenities is the primary role of Panchayats.
- Resource mobilization and management.
- Managing common properties.
- Managing natural resources.
- Proper channelization of functions and giving priority to urgent needs.
- Value neutral administration.
- To work for the cause of gender equality and solve gender related issues.
- To perform the obligatory functions.
- To give attention to the provision of quality education.
- To implement government schemes and programmes and monitor them through the Gram Sabha.
- To conduct regular Panchayat meetings and Gram Sabha meetings effectively.

The fifth question was about the roles and responsibilities of the Gram Panchayat. The participants were more conscious of the Gram Panchayat's roles and responsibilities than before. They mentioned the following :

- Convening the Gram Sabha meeting regularly.
- Proper implementation of Gram Sabha resolutions.

— Working towards creating a healthy society.
— To create awareness about the Gram Sabha.
— Sending all children to schools and *balwadis*.
— Proper implementation of plans/schemes of the government.
— Public grievance solving mechanism.
— Making the official concerned participate in the Gram Sabha meeting.
— Making women join various committees.
— Propagating the importance of Gram Sabha to the people.
— Working on consensus based public opinion in preparing annual plan.
— District administration has to recognize the resolutions passed in the Gram Sabha meeting.

With regard to making the people participate in the activities of the Panchayat to improve the Panchayat administration, they suggested the following :

- Mobilizing people to undertake environmental activities.
- Providing amenities like road, light, drainage, streetlight and involve the people in maintaining them.
- Involving the people in the maintenance of sanitary complex, burial and burning ground, library building, recreation building etc.
- Mobilizing the people through SHGs and youth clubs.
- Making the people participate in some crucial activities, e.g. maintenance of OHT, road, common property resources.
- Various committees may be organised and village people may be appointed to each committee, e.g. Peace Committee, Vigilance Committee, Health Committee, Education Committee, Planning Committee and Agricultural Committee.

The next question asked was about the maintenance of the common property resources. They gave the following replies :

- To start agriculture and small industries in the *poramboke* land.
- To implement wasteland development programme in the *poramboke* land.
- To grow plants for better yield for the Panchayats.
- Creating awareness among the public to safeguard public properties.
- To prevent encroachment on common properties.
- Auctioning and licensing the common property resources for proper maintenance — the amount realized can be used for welfare activities.
- Avoid exploiting resources like sand and mines.
- Hand them over to the village committee to manage the same.
- Making use of *poramboke* land with the help of the Revenue Department.
- Giving power to the Panchayat to punish the misusers and exploiters of the common property resources.
- Maintaining sacred groves.

To the next question on how one should go about augmenting the financial resources of the gram panchayats, the respondents gave the following suggestions:

- Revise taxes and ensure their prompt collection.
- People's contribution in the form of donations.
- Increase the number of small scale industries and plant trees on Panchayat land.
- Encourage and collaborate with SHGs to start economic activities.
- Increasing the number of fishing ponds.
- Find out the various government schemes and financial assistance available for Panchayat activities.

Most of the Presidents stated that their performance was affected due to lack of funds. After attending the training programme the participants were confident because now they knew about various sources and methods for increasing revenue.

The next question was about the steps that should be followed in the planning process. Most of the respondents gave suggestions, on what to do in the planning process and who should be included in the planning process.

- The Planning Committee should plan for basic needs.
- Plans should cover 5-year periods.
- Convening Gram Sabha to prepare a plan.
- The needs should be prioritized before detailing of the plan.
- The availability of resources must be taken into account.
- Identifying the beneficiaries in the Gram Sabha meeting.
- The Gram Sabha should be convened to prepare the plan.

The next question was about the attention given to equipping themselves to maintain accounts and records. Before the training 80 per cent of the Panchayat Presidents did not know the accounting procedure. They thought that the accounts are to be maintained by the Panchayat clerk. But now the Presidents know that they are responsible for properly maintaining accounts. They gave the following suggestions for proper maintenance of accounts :

- Maintain bills and vouchers properly.
- At least twice a month check entire accounts, i.e., 31 registers, bills and vouchers.
- Proper and regular collection of house tax and immediately deposit it daily in the bank, updating the passbook regularly.
- Proper inspection of activities/records.

With regard to social development, the respondents suggested that the following activities are to be undertaken in each village :

- Create awareness about girls education.
- Ensure child health care, immunization and nutrition.
- Ensure public health and sanitation.
- Ensure pre-natal and post-natal care.
- Maintain harmony in the society.
- Increase awareness about cleanliness among school children.
- Increase the number of self-help groups.
- Develop the weaker sections, particularly *Dalits* and women.
- Ensure proper understanding among various communities and caste groups.
- Work against the spread of dowry, female infanticide and foeticide.
- Sensitizing women regarding gender issues.
- Enhance the production of all agricultural commodities.
- Promote cultivation of medicinal plants.
- Utilize the assistance and guidance of NGOs, SHGs and other social organizations.

The next question was about how to develop leadership qualities. Their suggestions were as follows :

- Working for the whole community without bias.
- Ability to convince people.
- Self-confidence, listening capacity.

The next question was about the strategies to enhance the economic position of the Panchayats. The participants suggested the following :

- Increasing and collecting 100 per cent taxes properly.

- Establishing more number of SHGs and giving training to people to establish small business.
- Arranging self-employment for youth.
- Associating with organizations concerned with economic development such as NGOs.
- Increasing agricultural productivity in Panchayat lands.
- Ensuring the participation of the people in social development.
- Propagating the importance of family planning.
- Planning to make use of dry land and *poramboke* land.
- Developing orchards / groves and generating income through them.

The next question was about the means of developing the Adi-Dravida community. On this 90 per cent of respondents said that it is important to understand the problems of the Adi-Dravidas and SC people before trying to solve them. They also stated that it is important to implement government welfare schemes properly. Efforts must be made towards the creation of awareness about education, child marriage, environment and sanitation. These efforts should also focus on employment opportunities.

Next came the most important topic of women's empowerment. All the women Presidents were concerned about the upliftment of their own segment. They came out with important suggestions to empower women. They were :

- Forming SHGs to motivate women to achieve economic development through access to loan facilities.
- Creating awareness about women's education, child marriage and other related issues.
- Improving women's self-confidence to make them capable of decision-making.
- Implementing government's women's welfare schemes.
- Creating employment opportunity for the youth.
- Creating awareness about female infanticide as the first step towards its eradication.

- Creating awareness about health and hygiene, pre-natal and post-natal care, child education and child care.
- Creating awareness about rain water harvesting and toilet usage.
- Creating awareness among women about the implications of illicit liquor.
- Acting primarily President and only secondarily as executive authority.
- Regularizing the Panchayat electricity fees.
- Special plan for women's upliftment in the Gram Sabha.
- Training women in self-employment and educating them about the importance of family planning and small savings.
- Implementing special upliftment plan for destitute women and disabled ones.

The final question was about the list of priorities of Panchayat activities. On this 90 per cent of the respondents said that the following were their primary concern: women's development, children's development, education, toilet culture, avoiding of plastic, savings promotion, rainwater harvesting, ending child labour, health and hygiene.

The women Presidents' opinion about training was also asked. Most of the participants stated that they preferred 10 days training. A few participants were satisfied with a 7-day, another 10 per cent of the participants stated that they needed training once in 6 months. Most participants stated that they needed training once a year. Regarding the training programme they said :

- It was very much useful to women gram Panchayat Presidents to perform effectively.
- It gave them direction for taking bold steps in Panchayat activities.
- They gained knowledge about Panchayat administration and social development issues.
- They learnt the details of Acts and GOs.

- They gained knowledge about administration, audit, role and responsibilities of Panchayat Presidents.
- They learnt about financial and functional devolution of powers.
- They should be trained in the technical aspects also like how to harvest rain water, develop waste land etc.
- They should be trained in the technical aspects of small scale industries through exposure visits to all such units.

Finally, their way of functioning in solving issues was analyzed. Most of the participants took decision after analyzing the cause of the issues and the problem and also sought the assistance of the department concerned. Many worked on consensus to avoid problems and some sought the assistance of the police if the situation went out of control, e.g., communal conflicts, anti-social activities etc. A few said that there won't be any problem at all if there is more money. However, many of them were not satisfied with the powers given to them, because the powers were only on paper and not in practice. If more power were given they could solve any type of problems. Some said that the Gram Sabha was their operational ground to solve problems.

Everyone felt and indicated that the training which is being given now should have been given immediately after the election. When training information was given, representatives were reluctant to attend. It was only the Block Development Officers, who have driven the representatives to the training programme. After reaching here and listening to one or two sessions, they have realized the importance and worth of the training programme. Most of the occasions questions have been raised.

They said that the elected representatives have realized their roles, responsibilities, powers and even worth only after attending training programme. They understood the official procedures to be followed in Panchayat administration. They have learnt the art of establishing relationship with officials and the people.

Feedback from Participants about the Training (Men)

Sl. No	Category	Level of Satisfaction	PUD	DGL	TRH	SIV	RAM	THE	KAR	VIRD	Total	%
1.	Material Supplied	Fully Satisfied	237	120	212	158	207	65	88	240	1371	86.0
		To Some Extent	38	–	48	30	22	1	3	5	147	9.2
		Not Satisfied	–	71	5	–	–	–	–	–	76	4.8
2.	Classes Handled	Fully Satisfied	230	160	198	221	212	60	79	215	1375	86.3
		To Some Extent	45	31	53	21	17	6	12	30	215	13.5
		Not Satisfied	–	–	4	–	–	–	–	–	4	0.3
3.	Quality of Resource Persons	Fully Satisfied	201	164	204	236	216	59	82	238	1400	87.8
		To Some Extent	74	27	51	6	13	7	9	7	194	12.2
		Not Satisfied	–	–	–	–	–	–	–	–	–	–
4	Accommo-dation	Fully Satisfied	76	175	143	141	169	49	79	229	1061	66.5
		To Some Extent	117	16	36	80	40	17	12	16	334	21.0
		Not Satisfied	82	–	76	21	20	–	–	–	199	12.5
5.	Food	Fully Satisfied	154	111	209	131	201	57	76	232	1171	73.5
		To Some Extent	98	32	46	72	28	9	13	13	311	19.5
		Not Satisfied	23	48	–	39	–	–	2	–	112	7.0

(Contd.)

Table *(Contd.)*

Sl. No	Category	Level of Satisfaction	PUD	DGL	TRH	SIV	RAM	THE	KAR	VIRD	Total	%
6.	Classroom Facilities	Fully Satisfied	190	178	191	165	180	53	72	202	1231	77.2
		To Some Extent	85	13	8	44	24	13	19	43	249	15.6
		Not Satisfied	–	–	56	33	25	–	–	–	114	7.2
7.	Programme In charge	Fully Satisfied	207	184	232	203	205	57	83	227	1398	87.7
		To Some Extent	68	7	23	30	24	9	8	18	187	11.7
		Not Satisfied	–	–	–	9	–	–	–	–	9	0.6
8.	Cooperation of the officers	Fully Satisfied	173	115	173	192	208	58	81	243	1243	78.0
		To Some Extent	102	76	54	50	21	8	10	2	323	20.2
		Not Satisfied	–	–	28	–	–	–	–	–	28	1.8
9.	Duration of the programme	Fully Satisfied	179	180	248	204	205	51	91	173	1331	83.5
		To Some Extent	26	11	7	30	–	15	–	–	89	5.6
		Not Satisfied	70	–	–	8	24	–	–	72	174	10.9

Source: Computed.

Feedback from Participants about the Training (Women)

Sl. No	Category	Level of Satisfaction	DGL	TRH	PUD	SIV	RAM	THE	KAR	VIRU	Total	%
1.	Material Supplied	Fully Satisfied	90	118	118	80	105	30	24	68	633	79.2
		To Some Extent	15	13	22	20	11	9	20	30	140	17.5
		Not Satisfied	–	–	–	12	–	4	5	5	26	3.3
2.	Classes Handled	Fully Satisfied	102	113	121	98	110	36	29	88	697	87.2
		To Some Extent	3	18	19	13	6	5	14	15	93	11.6
		Not Satisfied	–	–	–	–	–	2	6	–	9	1.2
3.	Quality of Resource Persons	Fully Satisfied	104	114	123	83	98	40	35	93	690	86.4
		To Some Extent	1	17	17	17	18	3	10	7	90	11.3
		Not Satisfied	–	–	–	12	–	–	4	3	19	2.3
4.	Accommodation	Fully Satisfied	95	98	117	70	101	35	40	91	647	81.0
		To Some Extent	10	29	23	20	15	8	6	6	117	14.6
		Not Satisfied	–	04	–	22	–	–	3	6	35	4.4
5.	Food	Fully Satisfied	101	109	120	92	106	30	37	93	688	86.1
		To Some Extent	4	22	20	10	10	12	9	7	94	11.8
		Not Satisfied	–	–	–	10	–	1	3	3	17	2.1

(Contd.)

Table *Contd.*

Sl. No	Category	Level of Satisfaction	DGL	TRH	PUD	SIV	RAM	THE	KAR	VIRU	Total	%
6.	Classroom Facilities	Fully Satisfied	92	113	107	93	109	38	45	98	695	87.0
		To Some Extent	11	18	33	9	7	5	2	5	90	11.3
		Not Satisfied	2	–	–	10	–	–	2	–	14	1.7
7.	Programme in charge	Fully Satisfied	87	114	108	65	105	35	38	82	634	79.3
		To Some Extent	17	17	32	35	11	8	8	18	146	18.3
		Not Satisfied	1	–	–	12	–	–	3	3	19	2.4
8.	Cooperation of the officers	Fully Satisfied	97	109	113	109	103	30	39	53	653	81.7
		To Some Extent	8	22	27	03	13	13	7	40	133	16.6
		Not Satisfied	–	–	–	–	–	–	3	10	13	1.7
9.	Duration of the programme	Fully Satisfied	100	121	108	105	109	33	39	57	672	84.1
		To Some Extent	5	10	30	3	7	7	8	41	111	13.9
		Not Satisfied	–	–	2	4	–	3	2	5	16	2.0
Total											7191	100

Source : Computed.

They informed that their fear over Section 205 of Tamil Nadu Panchayat Act has gone. They felt that they have realized their potentialities and worth only through this training. They consider the Panchayat as a space for development. Till they attend the training they said they thought that Panchayat is a space for politics. They further informed that Panchayat officials should be given training. Panchayat institutions are in trouble because of the officials confusion over the new dispensation.

Here only they have realized how effectively the facilities could be utilized to achieve development. It provided self-confidence to the *Dalit* leaders. Absolutely they were not conscientized on social development. Only after training they have realized the implications and importance of social development.

Resolutions

It was a good moment when, in the feedback session, many of the Panchayat Presidents pledged that they would work first for social development issues. They assured the trainers that they would provide nail-cutter and toys to *balwadis*. They would ensure all services due to pregnant women from Health Centre and Primary Health Centre. They would achieve cent-per-cent school enrollment. They would work for reduction of school dropouts. They would see to construction of toilets for women and school and ensure their proper functioning. Some promised to provide chappals to school going children. Some promised that they would create awareness among the people about health and sanitation. They also resolved to eradicate the use of polythene bags in the villages. They further assured that they would create awareness among the people about the importance of water and how to conserve water. Finally, someone stated that they would take steps to reduce corruption. Another said that they would give importance to rain water harvesting and early childhood care.

Vision of the Women Panchayat Presidents

After three and a half days of intensive training in Panchayat administration, the women leaders were asked to build a vision by making use of the power the Panchayats are vested with. They envisaged the following :

— Forming SHGs and using them to clean the village.
— Creating awareness about personal hygiene among women.
— Constructing toilets in the *balwadis*, the school and every house.
— Providing drinking water supply.
— Planting trees on both sides of the Panchayat roads.
— Purchasing nail-cutters for distribution among *balwadis*.
— Making their Panchayats a model one.
— Stop using plastic tumblers in the Gram Sabha and use stainless steel tumblers.
— Provide basic amenities like roads, streetlights, drinking water facility, public health and sanitation.
— Construct houses for everyone so that no one is homeless.
— Leelavathy, President of Sitarur, said that she did not want to follow the example of the ex-Panchayat President.
— Planning and construction of park in front of the Panchayat office and in front of the school.
— Planning to construct hospital.
— Abolition of illicit liquor.
— Sending children to schools, *balwadis*.
— Cultivating habits of cleanliness among children and making them to use toilets.
— Cleaning the abandoned well and using it as drinking water source.
— Installing rain water harvesting structure in all homes and in public buildings.
— Planning to distribute one plant sapling to each house, particularly papaya saplings.
— Planning to abolish plastics in the Panchayat area.
— S. Lakshmi, President of Kannankudi Panchayat, pledged to make her Panchayat a clean, green and plastic-free village. She wanted to desilt the tanks with the help of the villagers not through any government schemes.

— Creating awareness about HIV and AIDS among all women in the Panchayat.
— Laying roads.
— Making the nurse stay in the village health centre the entire day and providing accommodation to her.
— Creating awareness about nutrition among pregnant women and children.
— S. Sasikala from Idaiakattur Panchayat said that she would increase the Panchayat revenue by producing organic manure.
— S. Maheswari, President of Maranadu Panchayat stated that women sell illicit liquor in her village and it is a very great task for her to change the minds of the women and to create alternative jobs for them. After attending the training programme, she is very positive that she will be able to bring about a change in the mindset of the women.

Veedu Panchayat, in Sivagangai District has a unique problem that many girls in that Panchayat are unmarried due to lack of bus facility. No one from other parts of the district can reach the Panchayat. Her first priority is to get bus facility from the district administration.

4

Trials and Triumphs of Panchayats

No doubt devolution of powers brings changes in the socio-economic life of the people in the rural areas. To get the better results from devolution the leaders, who are assuming responsibilities in different institutional structures, should have needed capacity to digest the powers devolved on them. Hence it is necessary first to work for proper devolution of powers. Equally it is so important to build the capacity of the leaders. After building the capacity, creating support structure to enable the leaders to overcome the obstacles and barriers in the devolution process. This being the continuous activities of the institute (Gandhigram Rural Institute), it had experienced a variety of cases of success in handling power and some were in struggle. Leaders apart from using devolved powers, assumed powers and responsibilities. By assuming responsibilities, they performed very well and made history of sorts. The struggles and success are to be brought to light as models are emerging for good governance from grassroots by overcoming all the barriers and struggles.

This chapter is the report of a workshop done with an objective of highlighting the success and struggles of the Panchayats.

I

INTRODUCTION AND INAUGURATION

The Panchayat Raj System, under the new dispensation, has been functioning in Tamil Nadu for the past seven years. News, observations, comments and criticisms relating to the Panchayats are proliferating in the media. Questions are being asked as to what the Panchayats have achieved, to what extent the women Panchayat leaders have taken up responsibilities and managed the institutions to deliver services and how *Dalit* leaders have perceived and performed their roles. To answer these questions a workshop was organized at Chennai to highlight the major achievements of the Panchayats, the major innovations introduced in the area of development issues, the problems and obstacles faced by the Panchayat leaders, the methodology adopted by the leaders to overcome barriers and obstacles, the problems faced by the elected women representatives and *Dalit* leaders in managing the Panchayats and the major issues which are to be tackled for the effective delivery of services by the Panchayats. It was a stock taking exercise wherein the achievements and the problems were analyzed with a view to evolving a strategy to create a more positive climate to enable the Panchayat leaders to perform their roles and fulfil their responsibilities effectively.

This exercise was programmed in a unique format. Instead of experts and administrators making speeches and observations or issuing comments and advice to the Panchayats, they were asked to listen to presentations by the Panchayat leaders and only at the end of every session an expert or an administrator was asked to make brief observations about the presentations and to suggest solutions to the problems posited by the leaders in their presentations.

One could notice a change in the dias arrangement also. The Panchayat leaders made their presentations under the Chairpersonship of a Panchayat leader. The expert, whether a secretary or a Director, had to sit only on the margin of the dias whereby the prominence of the Panchayat leadership was maintained. The Panchayat leaders took 95 per cent of the time in each session and only 5 per cent of the time was left for the experts' observations. Based on the presentations made by the Panchayat leaders and the observations of the experts/officials in the respective panels, an open house discussion was arranged in which a perspective could be evolved to take forward the Panchayats from their current stage to the next level. Finally, an action plan was evolved.

The programme started with a welcome address and introductory remarks by Dr. G. Palanithurai, Professor and Head of Political Science and Development Administration, Gandhigram Rural Institute, Deemed University. He briefly outlined the conditions under which the Panchayats are currently functioning. It is very difficult to generalize the functioning of PRIs in Tamil Nadu. It varies from district to district. Generally the climate is not positive. But in one respect Tamil Nadu is a model to other states. Devolution in Tamil Nadu is in an evolutionary stage. The Panchayat leaders always project their demands based on their track record of performance. In fact the Panchayat leaders are creating a conducive climate for devolution of powers. This workshop was intended to highlight their triumphs and the trials in the past seven years.

The programme was inaugurated by the Hon'ble Minister for Local Administration, Government of Tamil Nadu, Mr. C. Sampath. He openly admitted the fact that the Panchayat leaders have started addressing the development issues of the communities. The Chief Minister of Tamil Nadu has proclaimed that women's development is the priority of Government of Tamil Nadu and she has taken a series of steps to be implemented in the rural areas by the Panchayat leaders, particularly the women leaders. The Chief Minister of Tamil Nadu has declared that she will make Tamil Nadu the number one State in development. It is not a mere declaration alone. It has been followed up by a series of steps initiated by her. The Panchayat leaders have to play an important role in this endeavour. Social development issues can be tackled only by the Gram Panchayat Presidents. It has already been proved that the Gram Panchayat Presidents have done a commendable job with the powers and finances given to them, however limited they are, and several innovations have been introduced by the Panchayats.

Dr. Palanithurai highlighted the efforts of 'The Hunger Project' in building up model Panchayats in two districts, namely, Pudukkottai and Sivagangai. He observed that the Government is aware of the problems faced by the Gram Panchayat leaders and that they will be sorted out soon. Finally, he stated that this kind of workshop bringing the real leaders from the grassroots and making them explain the issues which have been faced in the field and the achievements of the Panchayat leaders is an eye opener for many to understand the transformation that has been taking place at the grassroots.

Following this Dr. Palanithurai released the report of the activities of the Rajiv Gandhi Chair for Panchayati Raj Studies and it was received by Mr. Madhavan of 'The Hunger Project'. A vote of thanks was proposed by Dr. V. Ragupathy.

II

INITIATIVES AND INNOVATIONS – I

Rainwater Harvesting, Setting up of Plastic Free Villages, Water Management and Sanitation and Non-Conventional Energy Sources

The resource persons (elected representatives) discussed the above themes based on their experience and experiments in the field. This session was presided over by a Panchayat leader, Ms. Rani Sathappan, the President of K. Rayavaram Gram Panchayat of Pudukkottai District. She observed that the Panchayat leaders, wherever they meet discuss the financial position of the Panchayats and the problems they face in Panchayat administration. But here the Panchayat leaders were to discuss new initiatives for major achievements and the major innovations they have introduced in their Panchayats. Powers and finances are the same for all the Gram Panchayat Presidents in Tamil Nadu. But a large number of Gram Panchayats have posted exemplary achievements. In this programme the focus was on the presentations of the Panchayat Presidents. Experts and officials were going to give their views on the presentations. After making this observation, she called upon the Presidents to make their presentations.

Ms. Sahaya Mary, the President of Kakkanur Gram Panchayat of Villupuram District, explained how she established a management system to solve the drinking water crisis in her Panchayat area. Her effort started from a tragic event that occurred in her village. When women were drawing water from an open well during a period of acute shortage of water, three of them drowned in the well. This prompted her to think and make society think of it and find a solution. She approached DANIDA for help. DANIDA promptly responded to her call. She fixed a flow control valve by which water supply was regulated. Thereby needed water was given to all and water was not wasted. She made the people accept the water regulations fixed by the Panchayat. The Panchayat kept the promise that water would be given to all. Water was equally distributed. When people got the assurance, they were ready to follow any norm fixed by the Panchayat. She constituted many committees in the Panchayat to manage the drinking water supply.

Mrs. Rani Sathappan herself explained the process by which she completely eradicated polythene from her Village Panchayat. It is now a plastic free village. She has become President for a second term and is continuing her activities. She became President of the Panchayat in the first period because of the reservation of seats for women. But now she has become President on her own by projecting her achievements in the first period and seeking the mandate of the people based on her performance. She scored a breakthrough in abolishing plastics and polythene in the Panchayat because of an accident that took place in the village. Nearly ten milch animals died after swallowing polythene materials dumped in dust bins. Taking this tragedy to the Gram Sabha, she discussed this issue with the people. Having convinced the people she evolved the norm that no one should use plastic articles in the Panchayat area and that individuals who violated it would be penalized. The people consented and the entire village has been made plastic free. For this exercise she got needed support from the SHG women leaders.

Yet another breakthrough she has scored in the Panchayat is establishing community action. There are two very big tanks in her Panchayat area. Normally such tanks are desilted and renovated by the PWD. But the PWD did not take care of the two tanks. She sent petitions to PWD. There was no response. She convened the Gram Sabha and discussed the issue with the members of the Gram Sabha. They passed a resolution that it should be reported to the District Collector for appropriate action. In the meanwhile they decided to desilt the tank on their own because the monsoon was approaching and before that the tank had to be desilted. The entire tank was desilted with the help of the community. The SHG women provided lunch to the people who worked in the tank. Community power was demonstrated for which the Panchayat President was responsible.

Mr. Choodamani, President of Karisalpatti Gram Panchayat of Dindigul District, brought a different experience from his Panchayat. In his Panchayat his predecessor had concentrated much on managing common properties by which the Panchayat could earn Rs.30,000 per year. He had made the community hall with adequate facilities, a marriage hall and fixed an affordable rent, through which the Panchayat now earns a minimum of Rs.20,000 per year. With the support of the community's contribution of Rs.1,00,000 he had constructed a very big tank and the tank now provides water for irrigation and drinking. He had started a campaign for sanitation even before the introduction of the 'Total Rural Sanitation Programme'. He had struggled a lot to sensitize the people on sanitation. By getting money from NGOs and other donor agencies he had constructed a few toilets for women and the women had been made to use these toilets. By doing this exercise he had created a toilet culture in one part of his Panchayat. Then the men had demanded such a facility and he took steps to provide toilets for them too.

The Panchayats' transparent activities prompted the people to have faith in the leader and the Panchayat. For any scheme the Panchayat can collect community contribution. Even in the implementation of the schemes this Gram Panchayat stands first. There is yet another unique feature. The formal Panchayat and the traditional Panchayat joined together and delivered services to the people. For drinking water management they evolved their own system which was accepted by the people. During the winter season water is supplied to individual houses and at many public points. During summer water is supplied only at common points according to a fixed time table which is convenient to the people. A committee monitors the supply. Thus a *pucca* water management system has been evolved.

All encroachments on common properties have been removed with the support of the community. Mr. Choodamani never approaches Police or Revenue officials. He has got the map from the Village Administrative Officer and he has identified the community lands and informed the public of the same through the Gram Sabha. The Gram Sabha has passed a resolution and authorized the Gram Panchayat to remove the encroachments. With the support of the community he has removed all the encroachments in his Gram Panchayat area. For rain water harvesting, within a week the Panchayat installed rain water harvesting structures in all the 811 houses. The formal Panchayat is always supported by the community for which the behaviour and performance of the leader is responsible.

Ms. Jesu Mary, the President of Michael Pattinam of Ramanathapuram District, narrated how the people of her Panchayat were struggling to get water to drink. There is no water source in the village. According to her, providing drinking water supply is the first priority in her village. She fought with the TWAD Board and got her village included in the TWAD Board drinking water supply scheme. When she attended a training programme, she was sensitized by the Secretary of Rural Development on the importance of rain water harvesting. She realized the importance of this new idea. But implementing the same in the village is not so easy. First, she created such structures in all the houses of the critics. After this the critics did not open their mouth to criticize the President. With the help of SHGs she installed the structures in all the 340 houses. It took several months for the people to realize the importance of this structure.

People started believing this scheme only when they saw the water level rising in their wells. After this they realized the importance of the structure. In the whole of the State it was the first Panchayat to create such a structure in all the houses in the Panchayat area. Ms. Jesu Mary got five other Gram Panchayat women leaders interested in this work and then five other Panchayats also carried out this work because of her influence. For all her success her opponents are responsible. Whenever she wants to introduce anything she discusses it only with them. She feels that critics are needed for healthy democracy. Critics' arguments will help the Panchayats to perfect the administration.

Mr. Shanmugam, the President of Odanthurai Gram Panchayat of Coimbatore District, presented his experience in innovations and initiatives. He maintained that for many of the ills in the rural areas the poor management system which we have developed for Local Bodies in Tamil Nadu is responsible. What we need at present is a people friendly management system to deliver services effectively and efficiently.

He started his work with water supply. He knew that enough water was available in the Panchayat area but it was not properly distributed. By merely changing the management system water could be ensured to all the families to the level of their need. First, he demonstrated his ability to change the system and its implications.

He informed the audience that it is a myth that people will not pay tax and other contributions. People will contribute money to common welfare to any level provided services are ensured. He cited his Panchayat as an example. When he took over the administration the annual tax collection was Rs. 23,000. Now it is Rs. 4,10,000. House tax collection is cent-per-cent. Through non-conventional energy sources he has provided street lights in the tribal areas by which he has saved Rs. 6,500 on electricity charges every month. For all major achievements people's participation is essential.

Mr. Panneer Selvam, the President of Keerapalayam Gram Panchayat of Cuddalore District, is unique in his performance. He got an award from the Government of Tamil Nadu for his achievements in providing individual toilet to every house in his Panchayat area. Public places and schools have also been provided with toilets with the support of DANIDA. It is the only Gram Panchayat fully covered under the sanitation programme in the whole of Tamil Nadu. His logic is that, to start any work, one has to go to the school, where all works can be done easily, because one can get active cooperation from the students. He further argues that a new culture for toilets can be easily developed among the students. Most of the works can be designed with the involvement of the teachers and the students. People will be convinced very easily if any one is in a position to demonstrate the results of any action. He introduced a number of innovations in cleaning the village and rain water harvesting. The

Panchayat has to preserve the green cover in each and every village. He maintains a clean village. It was possible because of the youth who created a healthy culture in the village that the village should always be clean and neat. For innovative works of the Panchayats the Government officials have to cooperate. Unfortunately officials at lower levels do not understand the value of the new Panchayat and its implications. For them Panchayats are an unwanted appendix. They have not changed their mindset and they behave as if Panchayats are under their control.

Mrs. Dhanapakiam, the President of Keelmavazangai Gram Panchayat of Villupuram District, explained her experience in solving the drinking water crisis in her Panchayat area. When she became the President of the Gram Panchayat she came to know the plight of the women in bringing drinking water to their houses from a long distance. In the same Gram Panchayat area half of the people were getting adequate water and in the other half they could not get water. The pipelines laid by the Panchayats were being damaged and the people had created pit taps. Even then they could not get adequate water. So she approached DANIDA. DANIDA insisted that the people should contribute money for drinking water supply. She explained to the people that at least a minimum contribution should be made. All the ward members took up the responsibility to mobilize resources. People contributed liberally to the tune of Rs.5,000. She started the work with the help of DANIDA. She formed committees to manage the water supply system. As a result water has been regulated through a flow control valve. Now water is available for all. There is no quarrel between the two regions of the Panchayat. Women are relieved from the drudgery. They are happy with the new arrangement. The timing of water supply has been fixed according to the need of the people. Payment for water supply is regular and without any delay. There is no defaulter. Delayed payment entails a fine of Rs.10. They have mechanics to repair the hand pumps. They never wait for such mechanics from the government. They attend to such work in their Gram Panchayat area and in other Panchayats also. Payment is made to the EB only from the amount collected from the people.

Yet another work done by the Gram Panchayat under her leadership is that waste has been turned into manure. In this Panchayat area there is no mosquito problem.

Following the presentations of the Panchayat leaders Dr. M.S. Udayamoorthy, the founder of the Makkal Sakthi Iyakkam, made an observation that he developed hope while listening to the major achievements of the Panchayat leaders that the existing socio-economic scenario in the rural area can be easily transformed by the Panchayat leaders. With the limited powers and resources, Panchayat leaders are able to achieve this much of innovations. Why does the State Government hesitate to give more powers and resources to Panchayats even after seeing these achievements? The women leaders who made significant contributions at the grassroots are going to be the models for MLAs and MPs. The women will make a difference in governance at the grassroots.

After the observation of Dr. M.S. Udayamoorthy, Thiru S. Ayyar, Director of Rural Development, Government of Tamil Nadu, complimented the Gram Panchayat Presidents on their achievements and accomplishments. Panchayat leaders are the real servants of the people. One can learn lessons from the Panchayat leaders as they perform their roles and responsibilities with so much of difficulties, obstacles and barriers. Officials do not have such barriers. Yet they have not achieved what the elected leaders have. He said that he learnt so many things only from the Panchayat leaders. In every Panchayat there is a Gram Sabha which is equivalent to Parliament. He further informed that he has instructed all the officials who are working in the Department of Rural Development to obey the orders of the elected leaders of Local Bodies. Officials are paid servants and not leaders. Officials at lower levels have to be oriented and trained properly. Steps are being taken to ensure the same. Local Bodies could be strengthened only by performance not by demanding power. Whatever power has been devolved has to be used for the benefit of the people. Power is to discharge responsibilities and to achieve development. The Government is willing to hear their problems and try to solve all those problems. A specific order has been issued to all District Collectors.

Periodical meetings between the officials and the Panchayat leaders will solve many problems.

III

INITIATIVES AND INNOVATIONS – II

Economic Development, Rural Housing, Public Distribution System, Solid Waste Management, Collective Action by the Community

Mr. Elango, the President of the Koothampakkam Gram Panchayat, while making observations in his presidential address in the third session, said that the dignity of every man and woman can be protected only when they are free from hunger. Hunger makes the individual surrender self-respect. The Constitution provides such protection and yet in reality three million people have no self-respect as they have to struggle for their food. Food security to the poor is the first task of the Panchayat. In our governance, poor people are the target audience for all kinds of activities. People are not being respected. The Panchayat system should not alienate itself from the people like the State and Central Governments. The Panchayat leaders should make the Panchayats people centric. The Panchayat leaders should look at issues from the perspective of the people. With these observations, he called upon Mr. Ramanathan, the President of the Nallukkottai Gram Panchayat of Sivagangai District, to make his presentation.

Mr. Ramanathan, a first generation leader, listed his activities in Nallukottai Panchayat. In his Panchayat area 47 families belonging to the Most Backward Class and 60 families belonging to the SC did not have own land for their shelter. He took steps to provide lands to both the SC and the MBC families. This was a major step which he took with the help of the District Collector. For SC people, he arranged to provide training in masonry by which all the SC people got employment opportunity.

Secondly, with the help of an SHG, the public distribution system was streamlined as the entire shop was given to the SHG. It earns a profit of Rs. 30,000 per annum. All needy people get provisions in exact measure. It is a major breakthrough that he has scored in his Panchayat.

Thirdly, in his Panchayat area there is no hut. All the houses have been made *pucca*. All the SC families got this facility and all the MBC families also got housing facility. SHG women have been trained in making paper cups. Forty families have been provided with loans to prepare charcoal for sale.

Mr. Durairaj, the President of Melachithalacheri Panchayat, narrated his experience in bringing a high school to his Panchayat area. The moment he assumed office he thought of establishing a high school as that was the demand of the people during the election. After three years of struggle he established a high school. He did not stop with it. He started his work only after the establishment of the school. Apart from attending to other Panchayat work he concentrated his attention on the school. As a result, for the past two years, the public school established by him has achieved a record 98 per cent and 100 per cent results respectively. People who previously sent their wards to nearby towns have now admitted their children to this school whereby he has enabled poor boys and girls to get education in their own village at minimum cost. He argues that he has a firm belief that if the schools are functioning properly, a new culture can be evolved favouring development.

Mr. Annadurai, the President of Maravamangalam Gram Panchayat of Sivagangai District, narrated his story of turning defeat into success in Panchayats by mobilizing the people for development work. In the first period he contested in the election but he was defeated. In the second election he won the seat. He is very popular among the people because of his timely action in preventing the Government from diverting water from a tank in his area to other places. The water from the tank which had been providing drinking water to 15 villages was diverted to other areas because of political interference. He objected to it. He was arrested and remanded for fifteen days. People mobilized themselves in this regard and because of the pressure exerted by the people he was released. He went to court and got justice for the people. The court has passed an order that the tank which provides drinking water to fifteen villages should not be used to provide water for cultivation. The Agricultural Cooperative

Society had become defunct in his Panchayat. He revived the cooperative society by collecting Rs.1,89,000 from the people. He is of the opinion that communities have got tremendous power. But, in our country, the leaders do not believe the community but they believe the bureaucracy and the State machinery. If the Government allows the Panchayats independence, they will do wonders. He carried out many schemes in his Panchayat worth several lakhs of rupees. But he does not consider these his achievements. Mobilizing the people to establish the supremacy of the community against the decision of the Government was his major achievement. He feels that the Panchayats of today are not Panchayats of the people. They are under the influence of the bureaucracy. How to redeem the Panchayats from the clutches of the bureaucracy is the matter to be carried at present.

Mr. Noor Mohammed the President of Sarkaraikottai Panchayat of Ramnad District, registered a breakthrough in his Panchayat by converting solid waste into saleable manure. He got the support of an NGO for this venture. By doing this work his Panchayat has earned Rs.13 lakhs. His village is clean and tidy. Now it is a clean village. If it is replicated in other Gram Panchayats, the entire rural area will be clean and the Panchayats can earn huge amounts of money. He also provided employment opportunity for a few in this venture. This was a major contribution made by him apart from attending to other Panchayat activities.

After this presentation, the session concluded with the observation of Mr. A.K. Venkatasubramanian, Former Secretary to Government of India. He stated that all good initiatives can be taken by the Panchayats. The Panchayats have to face a volley of problems. When the Panchayats are able to make this much of progress and achievements, everyone has to help the Panchayats. The Panchayat leaders have to make the Panchayats institutions of self-government. The Panchayat leaders by building their capacity, can change the existing administration. To support Panchayat institutions to make them institutions of self-government and good government, a movement has to be organized. This Panchayat movement has to support the Panchayat Raj System for the establishment of good governance.

IV

AGENCIES OR LITTLE REPUBLICS

Panchayat Plans, Devolution of Powers and Devolution of Finance

The next session was initiated by Mr. Elango with a brief introduction about the nature of the Panchayat system which we have developed in Tamil Nadu. If the Panchayat is a little republic, it should have the power to take decisions, to plan for development and to achieve economic development and social justice. First, to make the Panchayats little republics, the Panchayat has to evolve a plan with the participation of the people. Nowhere is it mentioned in the Panchayat Act that the plan has to get the approval of any higher authority. Plan documents can be approved at the Panchayat level. Hence every Gram Panchayat can develop a perspective development plan and it can get it ratified by the Gram Sabha. In Tamil Nadu, from Gram Panchayats to District Panchayats, no such exercise is undertaken. But, with the help of The Hunger Project, 13 Gram Panchayats in Pudukkottai District and 10 Gram Panchayats in Sivagangai District have embarked upon preparing a perspective plan. Their experiences are shared here.

Ms. Chinnammal, the President of Urathupatti Gram Panchayat, narrated how she developed a plan for her Panchayat. As per her perception, the Panchayat plan is nothing but a wish list. It is the desire of the people. Carrying out the plan is a difficult task as the Panchayat President has to find the money. Panchayats do not have adequate finance to carry out Panchayat works. Mobilizing the people for plan preparation is easy. They will participate in all common action. But governance is not in their hands.

The decision making power is not in their hands but in the hands of the officials. She further said that Panchayat leaders have to struggle a lot to fulfil the needs of the people. She felt that she had a dream and that dream had to be realized. To realize the dream planning was imperative. After the preparation of the plan, she first paid attention to the implementation of the Nutritious Noon Meal Scheme in the schools. She constructed a good kitchen for the preparation of food. She provided a nail-cutter to the *balwadi* to cut the nails of the students who come to the *balwadi* every Monday. The ration shop was run in a private house and it functioned as a private shop. She took steps to construct a building for the ration shop and shifted it to the new building and thereby made it a really public shop. She verified the list of people who were getting benefits through this ration shop. She then provided safe drinking water to the schools.

She reiterated that if people are mobilized and organized at the grassroots without any cleavage, the Government will abide by the wishes of the people. If the people are divided, the division will be used by the officials for their advantage. She said that she has realized the power of the people only through training. She stated that the Panchayat leaders have to be accommodating and should have patience in tackling the issues. The Panchayat leaders have also to be assertive, that too the women leaders. She reported that when the Panchayat clerk committed various lapses and mistakes, she dismissed him from the job. Pressure was exerted on her in the Gram Sabha. She convincingly presented the case and got it approved. The Government sanctioned a threshing floor and it was decided to construct the same in a place which was determined by Gram Sabha. But the MLA objected to it. She asserted that the decision was not taken by the President but by the people in the Gram Sabha. Finally, he accepted it. Panchayat leaders have to work under severe pulls and pressures. Unless they are capacitated, it is very difficult to manage the Panchayat. The plan is an instrument to mobilize people and pressurize the Government. So the Panchayat leaders need training continuously.

Ms. Veerakalaiarasi, the President of Veppankulam Gram Panchayat of Sivagangai District, explained her experience. Being a *Dalit*, she felt that the Panchayat had to look after the destitute, the ultra poor and women as they are the people unattended to. She felt that in Panchayat areas huge amounts of money are being spent through the sectoral departments as the Government has money. But felt needs are not attended to. That is why she took the initiative to plan for the development of the poor. She initiated steps to mobilize the people for which nine committees were formed. She first helped the ultra poor to get ration cards and ensured that needed provisions were supplied by the ration shops to them. Further she corrected the BPL list of beneficiaries. Yet another milestone in her Panchayat is that a school teacher working in her Panchayat school was transferred to another area. He was a good teacher who brought discipline to the school. Hence people from the Panchayat area demanded a retransfer for the teacher. She struggled a lot to get him again to the school and finally, she got a transfer for him. This incident made the people have faith in her and her capability. The plan preparation made the people come together, think together and act together. The planning exercise made the people think that the Panchayat is an affair of the people and not an affair of the Panchayat President.

Mr. Arumugam, the President of Edaiyathimangalam Gram Panchayat, had to put up a prolonged struggle to get back the common property from an individual. With the help of the village map got from the Village Administrative Officer, he identified the 28 acres and 58 cents common land used as a sand quarry by an individual. When this was disclosed among the people, it became a hot issue in the village. He used his influence to mobilize his supporters. He went to the officials including the District Collector but in vain. Finally, after a long struggle, he was able to meet the District Collector and convinced her in the matter and finally, she passed an order that the land has to be resorted to the Panchayat. As a result the land was retrieved from the encroacher and returned to the Panchayat and through the land the Panchayat has earned Rs. 21 lakhs. With the help of the community the tanks in the Panchayat area were desilted and deepened. He helped the Panchayat to establish a high school in the Panchayat area by mobilizing Rs.1 lakh from the people. According to his perception, if a Panchayat is able to mobilize resources from the commons and other taxable sources, the Panchayat can be self-sufficient.

Mr. Saravana Perumal, the President of Puvaloor Gram Panchayat, narrated his experience in Panchayat administration. In his Panchayat so far only landlords became Panchayat Presidents. He wanted to change the scenario by becoming the Panchayat President. He was defeated twice. This time he mobilized the poor and the backward classes. He won the election. He formed seven committees in the Panchayat.

Because of the periodical meetings a large number of people became friends of the Panchayat.

His first step was to put an end to alcohol in the Panchayat area. First, he mobilized the youth and women and he created awareness among them. He consolidated the youth force. With the help of the youth he destroyed the basic installation for the alcohol preparation. Totally the illicit liquor brewers lost nearly two lakh rupees. Subsequently he found alternative jobs for all those people. This he considered his major achievement in this Panchayat area. Other works were also carried out in the Panchayat area with the help of the schemes of the Government. According to him, power slowly moves to the middle class and the poor but these leaders have to be conscientized on social development issues.

Ms. Bhavani Ilango, the President of Merpanaikkadu Gram Panchayat, explained that she was totally opposed by a section of the menfolk. She was kidnapped by the opposition group. She escaped from them. She decided to move closely with the women. She formed 23 self-help groups and the SHGs helped the Panchayat to desilt a tank which provided drinking water to the entire area. Valuing the work done by the women in the tank as worth Rs.60,000, the officials who witnessed the contribution of the women helped the Panchayat by laying a pipeline for the entire area for the supply of drinking water.

She complained that the Total Rural Sanitation work was given to an NGO and it did not complete the work. Whatever work they have carried out, it is of poor quality. By using the power vested with the Panchayats, the President inspected the work and complained to the District Collector. Yet the deficiency was not corrected. There are a number of works carried out by the Panchayat. But why this work was given to an NGO is not known to the Panchayat President. She is confident that the Panchayats, especially women headed Panchayats, can achieve many more things if they get the support of the women in the Panchayat area. She felt that men have not changed their perception and attitude towards women even after seeing the transformation effected by the women leaders in Panchayats. They are to be conscientized on the problems of women and gender.

Mr. Abdul Waheed, the President of Parambur Gram Panchayat, lamented that the Panchayats and Panchayat leaders are treated as mere agents of the State Government and the Central Government. He said that there is no dispute over the money spent in the Panchayat area. But the question is whether the money spent in the Panchayat area has fulfilled the basic needs of the people. Even after the establishment of the Panchayat as an institution of self-government people's basic needs are not met, which means that the problems have not been sorted out.

Prof. K.V. Palanithurai, Full-Time Member of the State Planning Commission of Tamil Nadu, made his observation on the presentations. He said that powers have to be taken and used for the good of the community. One cannot expect powers to be given by someone from above. Planning is a mandatory duty that the Panchayats have to perform. They need not wait for the orders of the Government because it has been mentioned explicitly in the Act itself. The Panchayats have to develop their plan with the involvement of the people. As per the Act, every plan of each tier has to be approved at its level only. Hence the Panchayat plan has to be approved by the Gram Sabha. By preparing a plan document indirect compulsion could be exerted on the sectoral departments to spend their money on the needs indicated in the plan document. The planning exercise seems to be a complicated one. Once it is started, the problems can be easily sorted out. Further the planning exercise will alter the existing mode of activities from a supply driven one to a demand driven one. So the Gram Panchayat leaders need not wait for any orders from the Government to take the initiative to prepare the plan. They can take the initiative to prepare the plan for the development of the community.

V

TRIALS AND TRIUMPHS

Experience of Women Representatives

Ms. Ponnikailasam, the Chairperson of the Tamil Nadu Federation of Elected Women Representatives, narrated her struggle in developing a federation for elected women representatives. It was felt that a support structure should be created for women representatives to rescue them from their troubles. It was suggested in many fora. Finally, Gandhigram Rural Institute helped the women leaders to form a federation. She narrated the steps taken by the federation to orient the women leaders on various social developmental issues, particularly women and *Dalit* issues. It has developed the perspective that it has to act in a proactive manner. Whenever the government takes retrograde steps against the poor, women and *Dalits*, the federation will oppose them vehemently. She cited how on many occasions it openly opposed the moves of the State Government. When the Government of Tamil Nadu introduced the cheap liquor policy it was opposed by this federation and the policy was given up by the Government. She stated that Central and State Ministers and State level officials participating in their conventions and conferences offered useful suggestions to the federation. The federation has obtained a Government order for the women leaders to hold meetings with the District Collector whenever they face problems. The federation collects the demands of the elected women representatives and discusses them with the Secretary or the Director for Rural Development and sorts out the problems.

Ms. Venkateshwari, President of Gandhigram Gram Panchayat, explained how the federation consolidated its strength over a period of time. Many of the women leaders from Kanyakumari to Chennai have solved their problems through this federation. She pointed out that when a women leader was murdered in Urappakkam, no FIR was filed. The FIR was filed only after the intervention of the federation. There are many federations, namely, District Panchayat Leaders Federation, Block Panchayat Leaders Federation and Gram Panchayat Leaders Federation, but they are not visible. It is only the women's federation that is visible by its activities. For all this Gandhigram Rural Institute is responsible. The women leaders meet the Director of Rural Development frequently.

Ms. Salma, the President of Thuvarankurichi Town Panchayat, and a poet committed to women's upliftment, stated that she came to the programme with the assumption that these women leaders cannot speak out what they have in their records. Now, after listening to their presentation, she felt that she had not understood the reality. The impact of the training given by Gandhigram Rural Institute was visible in their presentations. She said that she now realized the importance of training and orientation. Till now she had thought that training is not an imperative but power and finance are. If power and finance were available achievements could be registered. Now she realized how with limited resources and powers the women leaders have achieved this much. Their capacity, their skill and their self-confidence and commitment brought about these achievements for which the training given by Gandhigram Rural Institute was responsible.

She asserted that the achievements scored by the women Panchayat Presidents are priceless and immeasurable as they have to face a volley of problems in the prevailing patriarchical structure. By overcoming all the barriers and obstacles, they have recorded such achievements. She pleaded that all Gram Panchayat Presidents' posts should be reserved for women as all the teachers' posts in primary schools have been reserved for women, since these women leaders have values, commitment, sincerity and needed perspective. She further suggested that the existing alliance has to be expanded. The alliance has to be extended to the media and other women's organizations.

Ms. Marudambal, the President of Panchampatti Gram Panchayat, said that Panchayat leaders can do wonders but their achievements are unnoticed. Women Panchayat leaders are always watched. There are people to criticize the women leaders. If a woman leader is able to score achievements, there are people to belittle the achievements. There are people to indulge in character assassination. Police cases are registered against her. She is able to withstand all pressures as she has gained confidence through the training. One advantage that the women leaders have in Panchayats is that they have more enemies than men and these enemies are the watchdogs of the Panchayats.

MLAs and MPs have no influence over the Panchayats headed by women. Everyone thinks that the women leaders have to obey the orders of the officials, MLAs and MPs, even if they are against the rules and provisions of the Act. But now, because of the federation of women leaders, this kind of attitude has changed. The continuous training and the alliance have changed the scenario.

Ms. Jamruth Beevi, the President of Devipattinam Gram Panchayat in Ramanathapuram District, narrated her entry into the public space for community development. She said that religion can never be a factor hindering achievement. She is a Muslim but she is loved by all both Hindus and Muslims. She has been re-elected to the Panchayat for a second term. She is of the opinion that to become a good leader one need not have formal education. Anybody can perform the role of the Panchayat President if he or she has commitment and moral values. She narrated her major activities in the Panchayat. As per her perception, one can claim an achievement if the activity is done on one's initiative. On that basis she said that she created a tank for a Hindu temple as many felt sad that there was no water tank for the temple. Further she took serious efforts to make her village clean. She took the initiative for solid waste management. She is very active not only in Panchayat activities but also in federation activities. She pays much attention to communal harmony. She personally intervenes and settles disputes. Her image among the public helps her to settle all these disputes. She has gained the faith and the confidence of the people by conducting the Panchayat administration in a transparent manner.

Ms. Kaliammal, the President of Therkkupatti Gram Panchayat, explained her struggle in Panchayat administration. She said that SC people are struggling in the society because of the divisions in the SC community. Where she won the election, another SC leader convened a meeting of 500 members and brought allegations against her and submitted them to the District Collector. It was written in the petition that the Panchayat leader has got Rs.5,000 as bribe to allot IAY houses to the poor. A witness was also prepared and she stated in the Collectorate that the President got the bribe. Ms. Kaliammal petitioned the District Collector to conduct an inquiry. Accordingly an inquiry was conducted and it was found that the allegations were false. Having failed in this attempt, the opposition group brought another trouble when the Panchayat

President took steps to provide water supply to a street by laying a pipe across their street. In this conflict the President's husband was assaulted and he was in hospital for one month. Since she belonged to SC the dominant caste groups created a ploy by selecting an SC group to work against her. It is sad that the poverty of the SC people can be exploited by anyone.

Mr. B.S. Raghavan, Former Chief Secretary, Government of West Bengal, made his observation, appreciating and complimenting the women Panchayat Presidents for their brave and wise actions in Panchayat administration. He said that the women leaders have acted with abundant common sense and a sense of commitment. Women leaders' actions will change the mindset of the bureaucracy and the menfolk. He said that the presentations made by the women Panchayat leaders from their experience were classic and thrilling experiences. It is true that they have come out of the house, occupied the public space, responded to the challenges, retained their values and emerged as models for emulation. He said that the women leaders are keen in attending to the problems of the marginalized. Really it is a second War of Independence. Women leaders regard this space as one meant for development. By their distinct behaviour and performance the women leaders have justified the reservation of seats for women. While going through the stories of the women one wonders how men can behave like brutes simply for power and money. To make Tamil Nadu the number one State in development the Panchayat has to work and women Panchayat leaders have to take the lead. With this observation he concluded his speech and asked the organizers to create a referable document out of the experiences of the women leaders.

VI

TRIALS AND TRIBULATIONS

Problems Faced by the Dalit Leaders

The next session was chaired by Ms. Pappa, the President of Athankaraipatti Panchayat. In her introductory remarks she said that the *Dalit* leaders have been facing a volley of problems at different levels. To glorify the existing order people give statistics to prove that many *Dalits* are in power in the Panchayat system and that their positions are proportionate to the population of the *Dalits*. Normally all the Acts passed in favour of *Dalits* are not used where they are needed. On most of the occasions they are misused. At the grassroots the *Dalits* are suffering a lot at the hands of the dominant caste groups. The sufferings of the *Dalits* can be felt or understood only by a *Dalit*. Other communities have only one suffering, that is, economic poverty, whereas the *Dalits* face human indignity also. To remove such indignity the *Dalits* need the support of many organizations and associations for which an alliance has to be formed.

After making this general observation, Ms. Pappa presented her problems in her Panchayat administration. When the Government sanctioned Rs. 2,60,000 for drought relief works, councillors and contractors asked the Panchayat President to hand it over to them for executing works. She refused to do so. As a result they influenced people at a higher level and stopped the funds. She fought through the federation to get the money released. She has given an interview to *India Today* about her agony. Even officials do not follow procedures and rules. Instead they join hands with the dominant elements. Audit is an evil weapon used by the officials to make the Panchayat leaders obey them. She said that she has to manage the dominant caste groups, officials and opponent groups. She is able to face them because of the training given by Gandhigram and the people's support. She is of the opinion that people of all castes are good as individuals. But they are misled by caste leaders and political leaders and they become dishonest for personal reasons.

Mr. Gopala Krishnan, the President of Brahmadesam Gram Panchayat, belonging to the *Dalit* community, narrated his struggle against the Block Panchayat Chairman who retained Rs.10,00,000 due to the Brahmadesam Panchayat Gopala Krishnan legitimately claimed the money for which he waged a relentless war against the Chairman. As a result he was put behind bars for fifteen days. Nobody took cognizance of the incidence. He faced it all alone. He performed his duties and responsibilities as per the provisions of the Tamil Nadu

Panchayat Act of 1994. He formed 40 SHGs in his Panchayat area. He inspected the noon meal centres periodically. He said that the leaders of political parties however democratic they are, want the *Dalit* leaders to obey their orders. As a result the *Dalits* have developed a suppression syndrome. When the *Dalits* are going to overcome this problem is a major question.

Elavarasan, the President of Shenbagarama Nallur Gram Panchayat in Tirunelveli District, brought to light his struggle in getting back the lands encroached upon by the Vice-President of the Gram Panchayat. The Vice-President, belonging to a dominant caste, had encroached upon Panchayat lands long back and cultivated the lands and used the drinking water for cultivating the lands. When Elavarasan became the President he got the map from the Village Administrative Officer and identified the Panchayat lands. He took steps to retrieve the lands from the encroacher. He tried his best to convince the Vice-President to restore the lands. Having enjoyed the benefits for long the Vice-President refused to do so and threatened dire consequences. Elavarasan went to the District Collector with a petition. The Deputy Collector inspected the area and oral instruction was given to the Vice-President to pay back the profit he had earned. On the same day the President was beaten up by the Vice-President and his brother. He lodged a complaint with the police. No action was taken. With the help of a CPI(M) lawyer he approached the Human Rights Commission. Following this the lands have been retrieved and handed over to the Panchayat. Now they are aiming at murdering this President. He has now approached the authorities for getting a gun licence for self-protection. No doubt reservation helps the SC and ST people to come up but they need a support structure. Gandhigram is doing this work. His plan is to contest in the Lok Sabha election.

Ms. Kala, the President of Noothulapuram Gram Panchayat, explained that, as a woman, she has to face a volley of problems in the Panchayat. If the elected woman representative belongs to the *Dalit* community the problems are insurmountable. Throughout the State Presidents' positions in Gram Panchayats have been reserved for SC and ST people proportionate to their population. When these positions are reserved for SC and ST people, the dominant caste groups immediately design to elect a

Vice-President by whom the elected *Dalit* leaders can be controlled. These *Dalit* Presidents face problems not because of the people but because of the Vice-Presidents. These Dalit leaders are not treated as representatives of the people. Officials at higher levels treat the *Dalit* leaders with respect but, at the lower levels, they face human indignity. The Secretary and the Director of Rural Development offer a seat to a *Dalit* President but the Block Development Officer does not. Officials have established close linkage with the dominant caste group leaders. For many of the problems of the *Dalit* leaders the officials are responsible. She pleaded that when a Gram Panchayat leader's position is reserved for SC and ST people, the Vice-President's post should also be reserved for them.

Mr. Christudoss Gandhi, Secretary to Government, Tamil Nadu, while making his observations, appreciated the *Dalit* Gram Panchayat Presidents for striking a positive note. He said that so far, wherever *Dalit* Panchayat leaders organized their meeting, they used to lament upon their woes and problems. But here the *Dalit* leaders have listed their major achievements and innovations. Further they have explained how they have achieved all these in the Panchayats and how they have overcome the barriers. It is a lesson to other *Dalit* Gram Panchayat leaders. The Government should also learn from these experiences how it can help the Presidents to achieve better results. *Dalit* Panchayat leaders are performing their role and responsibilities with several constraints and barriers. On most of the occasions they live under mortal fear. Panchayat leaders register complaints but they are not attended to. The existing official machinery is working under the direction of dominant groups. When protection is given to Mr. Thogadia of the VHP, why is protection not given to *Dalit* Panchayat Presidents? In what way is Mr. Thogadia superior to a *Dalit* Panchayat President or a *Dalit* President inferior to Mr. Thogadia. When a government is not able to conduct election properly to three Gram Panchayats in Madurai District, why does it use Section 205 against *Dalit* Panchayat Presidents?

Dalit Gram Panchayat Presidents have to develop confidence to face the crises in Panchayat administration. *Dalit* Panchayat leaders have to form their own organization to discuss their problems and to evolve strategies to overcome the same. They have to form alliances to get their problems solved. In Tamil Nadu more than 3000 Gram Panchayats are under the leadership of *Dalit* Panchayat Presidents. They have to perform their role as Panchayat leaders and as *Dalits* to attend to *Dalit* problems also. *Dalit* Panchayat leaders have to build their skill and capacity to manage the Panchayats. It is fortunate that Gandhigram Rural Institute has taken up the responsibility of not only building the capacity of the Panchayat leaders but also of building wider alliances to get the support of all sections. Media support is necessary for the *Dalits*. The climate is positive now and it has to be used by the *Dalit* leaders. *Dalit* Panchayat leaders have to devote more time to the management of common property resources. They have to retrieve the commons from encroachments and not allow the natural resources to be exploited by business houses. *Dalit* leaders have to build their skill and alliance to triumph over their problems and to perform their constitutional duties and responsibilities.

VII

MANAGING PANCHAYATS

Common Property Resource Management and Environmental Protection

Ms. Chandrika Sarvesan, the President of Siruthondanallur Gram Panchayat of Ramanathapuram District, brought to light the condition of women leaders. She said that the women leaders face an array of problems in the public space. As they work in the community, on most of the occasions, the behaviour and the performance of the women leaders are seen against the backdrop of the community's laws and not of constitutional laws. They are not MLAs and MPs to work far away from the community. As everyone is aware the eye of the public on women is not always positive. Women leaders have to work under severe stress and strain. In Tamil Nadu if women leaders, especially at Gram Panchayat level, are able to work to this level and win appreciation from all quarters, it is because of the training provided by Gandhigram Rural Institute. Training in Government parlance is threatening the Panchayat leaders by listing 'don't dos'. But in Gandhigram training is extending support, bringing out the potential of women, rescuing the women leaders whenever they are in trouble. Now a stage has come to stand on their own feet by forming a federation of elected women representatives. Even for this exercise Gandhigram has done a good deal of work for which the federation has to be thankful to Gandhigram Rural Institute.

Ms. Suganya, the Gram Panchayat President of Vellimalaipattinam from Coimbatore District, focused her presentation on the role of women leaders in the Gram Panchayat. She narrated her personal experience. She started her work from the children and the women as one can show better outcome through such activities. She first created awareness among the SHG members about the importance of children. It was only the SHG members who took the initiative to take care of their children in terms of health, cleanliness and education. Now one can see in her Panchayat the way the *balwadi* is maintained and the school is maintained. Even *Dalit* children are clean and neat and they are regular in attending school and they use the toilets.

She said that minor minerals are being exploited by middlemen, brokers, politicians and the mafia. The Panchayats are totally sidelined. The Panchayat leaders have to take necessary steps in this regard. Sand is being over-exploited by these groups. As a result, villages face severe environmental degradation. The women leaders federation is taking keen interest in these issues. One should realize the danger involved in it as the mafia is doing this.

Ms. Eswari, the President of Appipalayam Gram Panchayat of Karur District, narrated the problems in her Panchayat. Environmental issues have become acute and as a result the people have lost their source of drinking water. Some people in the name of development have spoiled the natural resources. In the Karur area people have sold their lands to industries which manufacture dyes. The waste coming out of the factories has completely spoiled the drinking water source. What can the Panchayat do in this regard? As a Panchayat President she started her agitation against all these industries. Everyone is aware of what type of trouble the industrialists can give. Officials normally support the powerful. The officials, as per the instruction of the industrialists, took action against the President under Section 205. She brought it to the notice of the Government. The Government instructed the officials to take steps to provide protection to her. Yet they have done nothing. But the people have extended support to the Panchayat to fight against such atrocities.

Yet another problem confronting the Panchayat is sand quarrying. A powerful mafia is involved in it. They violate all the norms and rules. They even threaten the higher officials. But she is fighting against the mafia with the support of the people. Officials always support the mafia due to mortal fear. The Panchayat can save the poor women and nature with the active support of the people.

Mr. Seran, the President of Thiruvasi Gram Panchayat of Tiruchirapalli District, said that he has been in struggle for the past two years to protect the sand from illegal mining. Everyone knows that in Tamil Nadu a mafia is involved in this work with political backing. That is why on many occasions even officials have been murdered by the mafia gang. He is fighting against this illegal mining of sand in his Panchayat area. He brought it to the notice of the people and discussed it in the Gram Sabha. He got the approval of the Gram Sabha to take action against this mining. While fighting against illegal mining, he has to fight against the officials also. The officials support the mafia and, as a result, 7½ lakh rupees due to the Panchayat has not been released to the Panchayat. His cheque power has been taken away. He is fighting against such actions of the officials with the help of the people. He has built up an alliance with the media and the media is reporting periodically the problems involved in this struggle. He pleaded with the participants to extend their support to such a kind of struggle. A large number of Panchayat Presidents are facing such problems.

Dr. V. Ragupathy, a specialist in Common Property Resources Management, said that the Panchayats, along with the community, have a great responsibility to protect the commons as they are the lifeline of the poor. He narrated how in Goa a

Gram Panchayat President fought against a multinational company and successfully removed it from the Panchayat area with the help of the judiciary and the people. The commons have been managed by the communities over centuries. They have evolved a management system for the commons. Hence the Panchayat leaders should take necessary steps to protect the commons and they should seek needed powers from the State Government in this regard.

VIII

MEDIA AND GOVERNANCE AT GRASSROOTS

A panel of experts from the media devoted time to the linkage between the media and grassroots governance. Mr. Maalan, the editor of *SUN New,* responded to the queries of the Panchayat leaders. He admitted that the media has not given sufficient coverage to the activities of the grassroots institutions though they work for development. The media generally covers news on State and Central politics. He said that this neglect is not wanton. It is due to the absence of sensitivity on the part of the media to grassroots institutions and their functioning.

Now there is a market potential for any new magazine carrying Panchayat news exclusively as lakhs of people are positioned in Panchayats as leaders. Private ventures or even Panchayat leaders can join together with research institutions to launch a community journal carrying news from the Panchayats. But nobody takes up such ventures. The Panchayat can spend Rs.50 per month and receive 12 issues from which it can get information relating to administration, innovations, schemes and programmes of the government, success cases and struggles. It is possible now. Either an individual or a group or an institution can do it. Silently a revolution can be started at the micro level for social transformation.

Ms. Salma, a town Panchayat President and poet well-versed in the affairs of the media, highlighted the power of the media. She said that the media can make and unmake things. The media's intervention and information dissemination can bring about a sea change in the society. Now, at the grassroots level, individuals and institutions need information regarding governance, management, administration, innovations etc. The media has to be brought into the domain of grassroots governance for which the media has to be sensitized.

Dr. Markandan, former Vice-Chancellor of Gandhigram Rural Institute, stated that the media plays a crucial role in bringing socio-political and economic issues to the public for dissemination and for action. In a democracy the fourth estate has an important role to play. He regretted that the media in India pays too much of attention to politics but little to development. It focuses more on non-issues than on issues. In many newspapers views are not expressed. The media lacks analysis. It merely provides information. He concluded his observations with a plea to the media to devote more coverage to news from the grassroots than that from the capital cities and towns.

IX

OPEN HOUSE DISCUSSION

An open house session was chaired by Dr. G. Palanithurai, Chairperson of the Tamil Nadu Council of The Hunger Project. He urged that the Panchayat leaders should move from the "I govern you participate" mode to the "we govern and we participate" mode. Now the Panchayat leaders leave the Panchayats in the hands of the officials and carry out activities as per the instructions of the officials. This trend has to be reversed.

There is yet another trend which affects the people and which has to be changed. People are the prime movers in any democracy but, in India, they are the receivers of government benefits as beneficiaries by submitting petitions. There is no culture in India to respect the people. The primary task of the Panchayat is to deepen democracy. The Panchayat has to work for achieving economic development and social justice. From the two-day deliberations one can judge where Panchayat institutions stand and how they move towards what target and goal. The new democracy at the grassroots must evolve a new culture.

Following this observation, many of the participants raised certain issues which were discussed at length. They are summarized hereunder.

- Now the Panchayat is leader centric and it should be made people centric.
- The Panchayats function only as agents to carry out the schemes of the Central and State Governments. They should be made institutions of self-government.
- The Panchayats should be given powers as they were given in the 1958 Panchayat Act of Tamil Nadu.
- Linkage among the three tiers of the Panchayats has to be created.
- The Panchayats have to be given untied funds every year up to Rs.5 lakhs for social development activities.
- Any scheme or programme should be carried out only with the approval of the Gram Sabha.
- Computer facility has to be given to all Gram Panchayats.
- MLAs' and MPs' funds have to be done away with.

X

VALEDICTORY

Finally the valedictory function began with a formal welcome address by the Registrar of Gandhigram Rural Institute. While welcoming the gathering he said that India has 320 million tons of agricultural waste which is equivalent to 220 million tons of coal and through which 16000 megawatt power can be generated. From the waste we can make wealth. But we are not doing so now. Gram Panchayats have started this kind of innovation in the Panchayats. This is a model to State and Central Governments.

Dr. John Coonrod, Vice-President of the Global Board of The Hunger Project, briefly touched upon where one has to concentrate to achieve development of human society. While listening to the presentations of the Gram Panchayat Presidents, particularly the women, he was deeply touched and impressed. Human Development is the primary requirement for all development activities. It has to start from women and children.

While considering the condition of women and children in India, one perceives clearly that it has to be changed, for which a strategy to be evolved. He explained the malnutrition cycle. He stressed the need for the Panchayats to attack all these issues at the grassroots through the Panchayats.

Ms. Rita Sarin, Country Director of The Hunger Project, said that she wished that the women leaders of Bihar and UP should become like the leaders of Tamil Nadu in terms of skill and capability. Panchayat leaders can make a difference in the life of the poor. The elected women representatives have their own vision which has to be realized. Women leaders have to address the issues of women and children vigorously. They have to set themselves as models in this regard.

Dr. V. Palanisamy, State Election Commissioner, in his valedictory address, complimented Gandhigram Rural Institute on its multi-faceted activities to build the capacity of the leaders and conscientize the people on development and the elected representatives of the Local Bodies on their excellent performance in achieving economic development and social justice. He felt that needed support has to be extended to the Panchayats for their effective and efficient functioning. There are certain issues which are to be addressed by the government. These will be attended to by the State Government for which the State Election Commission will take the initiative. While devolving powers one has to consider the capacity of the lower level institutions to digest the devolved powers. From the presentations one can easily come to the conclusion that the leaders at the grassroots in Tamil Nadu possess the needed capacity to, digest the powers. Women leaders have excelled in their performance and they have outwitted the men. To make Tamil Nadu the number one State in development, the Panchayats have to be equipped adequately. The State Election Commission is making earnest efforts to remove all the barriers to the smooth conduct of elections. He appealed to the participants to express their views on the system of election which is in vogue. Based on the comments of the elected representatives, suggestions will be prepared for Government of Tamil Nadu for adoption.

The programme came to an end with a vote of thanks proposed by Dr. S. Narayanasamy, member of the State Council of the Tamil Nadu branch of The Hunger Project.

Interferences from this Workshop

- Panchayat Presidents have proved that Panchayats can perform better provided the Panchayat leaders have commitment and capacity.
- Women leaders have shown the way to others in innovations and developed strategies to build alliances to overcome barriers.
- This kind of exercise will instill hope in the opinion makers to convince the policy makers that Panchayats can perform beyond expectations.
- Performers mostly have the perception that decentralization is for development and social justice.
- Women leaders consider the Panchayat a space for development and not a space for politics.
- Decentralization has brought to light the social problems which affect the process of social transformation.
- Panchayat leaders have realized the importance of training and continuous flow of information in Panchayat administration.
- Panchayat leaders have gone for media alliance through which the struggles and successes are brought to light for larger dissemination.
- People's participation and micro level planning are considered pivotal for the success of Panchayati Raj Institutions.
- Women Panchayat leaders are conscious of social development issues and they are concientized on the issues of children and women.
- Community aspirations and practices have been amplified in Panchayat administration.
- Women leaders have developed the practice of meeting the higher officials periodically and sorting out their issues without much trouble.

For Policy Makers

— Steps can be taken to devolve more powers and finance to the local bodies to tackle many of the issues of social development.

— Micro level planning can be initiated by the government by which the trend can be reversed from supply driven mode to demand driven mode.

— Periodical meeting of officials with the Panchayat leaders will enable them to perform their roles and functions better.

— Untied funds can be given to Gram Panchayats for initiating social development activities.

— The mindset and the behaviour of lower level officials working in the Panchayati Raj Institutions have to be changed through sensitization and conscientization.

— Gender sensitization has to be provided for all officials, particularly those who are working in Panchayati Raj Institutions.

— Panchayats and State Governments are in a win win situation as the Panchayats use their maximum potential to achieve results in the Panchayats. As a result the level of development activities goes up and thereby the State Governments' position in achieving development will also go up.

— Wherever District Collectors are positive towards the Panchayats and personally work with the Panchayats, the Panchayats face less problems.

— Wherever District Collectors leave the responsibility to the Assistant Director of Panchayats, the Presidents are threatened and kept away from the District Collector and they face a volley of problems.

For Development Organizations

— Creating a support structure for the women and the Dalit leaders and helping them to perform their roles and responsibilities.

- — Helping them to initiate activities for evolving a micro level plan for the development of the Gram Panchayat.
- — Helping the Panchayats to identify the people who are wallowing in abject poverty and work for the development of those families by constantly monitoring them.
- — Conducting periodical refresher courses for the Panchayat leaders, updating the latest GOs and programmes of the government.
- — By bringing together the achievers and leaders who have struggled opportunities are created for spreading success messages.
- — Organizations working sectorally in the rural areas can work with the Panchayats for effective delivery of services and to get better results from the activities.

In Tamil Nadu through the new opportunity devolution is evolved and not imposed. This evolution of devolution takes places in a natural way through peaceful means by projecting the success of the devolution. It has started moving from the old concept "I govern you participate" to "we govern and we participate".

5

Observations and Conclusion

Panchayat leaders have different socio-economic backgrounds and levels. It is true that power has gone down to even the ultra poor. Once the Panchayats were under the control of the rich and Zamindar families. Now the really poor have come to power. Further, because of the reservation of seats for women and *Dalits*, power has gone to the last man also. No doubt this is a positive step. But do they have the capacity to manage these institutions? The poor who have come to power find it difficult to manage these institutions not only because of lack of skill and ability but due to the problems that prevail in the social system. Apart from these problems, the Panchayat leaders have to manage the officials who are used to dominating the elected leaders. Gram Panchayat Presidents who hail from higher castes and dominant castes carry weight when they go to offices of the government but in the case of others beneficiary treatment is given in government offices.

Panchayat Raj is a system. But in reality it is not so. It is inferred from the Panchayati Presidents' reports that practices vary from one district to another. Thus the Panchayat Raj performance is always linked to the support extended by the District Collector as Inspector of Panchayats. Wherever the Panchayati Presidents are fully aware of the Panchayati system they assume responsibilities. They know the value of the participation of the people. They mobilize the people for common action.

Information is a key to administration but the Panchayati Presidents work in the Panchayats without adequate information about the Panchayati Act, rules, government orders and government schemes for rural development. Only during the training it was found out how the Panchayat Presidents are handicapped. All this information has been provided as a package.

While imparting training it was found out that many of the State Acts contradict the provisions of the Panchayati Act of Tamil Nadu. They are to be amended. Officials who are working in the Panchayat Raj System are not sensitized on the importance of decentralized governance. Training should be given to officials including the District Collectors on Panchayats. Several interventions by District Collectors have been questioned by the court and higher authorities as they have not followed the procedures. There are variety of critical issues which are to be tackled by the State Government.

Normally the Panchayati leaders lament about the powers needed for the Panchayats. But they really do not know how much of power has been conferred upon the Panchayats. The conferred powers have not been fully utilized by the Panchayat Presidents. There are Panchayat Presidents who have crossed the boundary and assumed certain responsibilities and carried out activities.

Panchayat Presidents are doing several innovations in Panchayat management. Panchayati leaders who have got commitment and faith in the community have demonstrated their ability to deliver services very effectively to the people and the community is totally involved. They administer the Panchayat in a transparent manner and win the recognition of the community. It is inferred from the interaction with the Panchayat Presidents that Panchayats need very little. The problem is that felt needs are not met as the resources are allocated for specific activities. Micro level planning is another imperative which is totally dormant. A series of steps have to be taken to set right the system. The recommendations arrived at are given below :

- Acts which contradict the provisions of the Tamil Nadu Panchayati Raj Act of 1994 have to be identified and suitable amendments have to be made.
- All officials have to be trained and sensitized on the New Panchayati Raj System. Many a time officials at lower levels administer the Panchayat without

understanding the Act and the rules. As a result the Panchayat lands in trouble.

- For proper Panchayat administration, an administrative manual has to be prepared and published.
- All Government Orders pertinent to Panchayat administration have to be compiled and kept in all Panchayat offices as it has been done in Pudukkottai District.
- A review has to be undertaken of the actions taken by the District Collectors on Panchayat leaders by using Section 205 of the Panchayat Act of Tamil Nadu, 1994.
- There is no prescribed mode of handing over and taking over charge of Gram Panchayat administration after the election to the Panchayat. Records created by the previous Panchayat administration are not handed over to the newly elected President.
- A sizeable portion of common properties has encroached upon by influential individuals. They are to be recovered and that can be done by the revenue department as a special drive. Though a GO has been passed no VAO has handed over the village map to the President and the properties of the Panchayats have not been shown to the Gram Panchayat Presidents. Higher officials of the Revenue Department, preferably the Secretary for Revenue, has to instruct the VAOs through an order that all *poramboke* lands of the Panchayats have to be identified and shown to the Panchayat Presidents and that the village map has to be given to the Panchayats.
- House tax levy and collection have to be made rigorous and periodic revision has to be enforced. In most of the places the Panchayats want direction from the State Government to enhance the house tax as the Panchayat is seen as leader centric.
- Minor minerals revenue must go to Gram Panchayats. But now the matter is in court. Nobody has taken action in this regard. As a result minor minerals are being lifted for the profit of mafia gangs. The State

Government has to take the initiative to expedite the case in the court.

- Drinking water supply is going to become a difficult task in the years to come in the rural areas. There is no proper water management system and no regularization of illegal tap connections. All these problems have to be solved. Water policy and water regulation rules have to be evolved.
- The Panchayats have to take the initiative for micro level planning which will turn the activities from a supply driven mode to a demand driven one. Huge amounts of money have been spent in the villages by different agencies but the demands of the people in the Gram Sabha meetings are unmet. Departments and representatives of the people has spent the money at their disposal in the rural areas as per their wish and perception. To avoid this kind of wastage, micro planning has to be initiated and thereby planned activities have to be carried out by pooling the resources of all the Departments and the representatives of the people.
- Panchayat leaders have to be sensitized on social development issues. Awareness has to be created among the leaders about the status of rural areas in terms of social development.
- The Panchayats have to keep the EB cards in the Panchayat office. Panchayat leaders have to monitor the electricity consumption and meter reading. In many Panchayats, the cards are not available in Panchayat office and the Panchayat Presidents are not aware of the EB expenditure. The EB cards are in the EB office. Wherever the Panchayat leaders are sensitized and conscious about the expenditure they take action to reduce electricity consumption by fitting tubes in the streetlights and removing sodium vapour lights and regulating the water supply.
- It should be made mandatory that all development works funded by sectoral departments or the Centre or the State Governments and carried out in the Panchayat area

should be undertaken with the approval of the Gram Sabha. Panchayat Presidents are being criticized for not convening the Gram Sabha meeting seriously as the Gram Sabha attendance is poor. When the proceedings, resolutions and demands of the Gram Sabha are not seriously considered by the officials, MLAs and MPs, how can one expect the people to participate? People know that the District Collector is powerful, the PO, DRDA is powerful, the MLA has Rs.77 lakhs and MP has two crore rupees at his/her disposal and hence people meet all these representatives and the District Collector.

- Issue of birth, death and community certificates should be vested with the Panchayat administration. Certificates issued by the Panchayat should be produced for public verification.
- Funds earmarked for Panchayat activities should be directly given to the Panchayats.
- The District Planning Committee has to take the initiative for evolving the perspective development plan of the district. The District Planning Committee has been constituted but there is no work assigned to the committee. A District Panchayat Secretary has been appointed as Planning Officer but no planning work has been entrusted to him. Manuals have been prepared for planning, training has been conducted for officials in multi-level planning and yet there is no systematic planning.
- Officials should not allow the husbands of the women Panchayat Presidents either to participate in the official meetings or to sign any of the papers which are to be signed by the elected women representatives. In many of the districts lower level officials encourage the male family members of the women leaders to attend meetings or carry out activities. If officials are very strict in this regard either genuine women will emerge as leaders or men of the women leaders' family will change their attitude. Most of the women leaders insist

that a very strict order has to be issued to the officials not to encourage such a trend.

- For each Panchayat an untied fund up to a maximum of Rs.5,00,000 can be given with an instruction to spend only for economic activities, particularly employment generation and social development as it has been done in Kerala.
- For women and *Dalits* a special development component plan can be developed.
- Panchayati Raj Institutions require one State level Director to look after the functioning of Panchayati Raj Institutions as per the recommendations of the Swaminathan Committee. To make the Panchayati institutions from the District Panchayat to the Gram Sabha institutions of self-government, their functioning has to be monitored and corrective steps have to be taken then and there, for which state level officer has to be given charge of these institutions.
- The revenue from forestry has to come to the Panchayats. But no effort has been made in this regard. Panchayat leaders have repeatedly made a plea to get the dues to the Panchayats.
- Village Panchayats which are very near to industrial estates can get a lot of revenue through house tax, building tax, layout approval and plan approval. But now this does not happen in many cases because the Panchayat Presidents are not aware of the rules. In certain cases the rules are misused to the advantage of leaders.
- Cheque transactions can be avoided and the entire grant can be sent to the bank account of the Panchayats for all activities by which corruption can be eliminated since all Panchayats have bank accounts.
- Still a major portion of the common properties are with the traditional Panchayats. They get huge amounts of revenue from common properties but they pay very little to the Gram Panchayats. In many places the auction of commons is taken by the traditional Panchayats at a nominal rate and the same commons are reauctioned for

a huge sum. The traditional Panchayats keep the balance amount after remitting the dues to the Panchayats. In many places the traditional Panchayats work in tanden with the formal Panchayats. In some places they are at loggerheads. This is to be studied seriously and appropriate action has to be taken.

- All sectoral departments have to inform the Panchayat Presidents about the schemes and programmes they are going to carry out in the Panchayat area. The Panchayats are given powers, not to decide about the works to be carried out, but to help the sectoral departments to implement and carry out the activities. But at present the sectoral departments do not even consult or inform the Panchayats about the programmes being carried out in the Panchayat areas. If annual plan preparation is done in every Panchayat, the sectoral department activities can be integrated with the plan of the Panchayats.
- Whenever licence is issued for quarrying, a copy of the licence should be sent to the Panchayat.
- Panchayat leaders at the Gram Panchayat level feel that the District Collectors have to convene a meeting of Gram Panchayat leaders once in a while and help the Panchayat administration by eliminating hurdles created by lower level officials. It will help not only the Panchayat administration but also the district administration for speedy implementation of schemes and programmes. Wherever the District Collector establishes direct contact with Gram Panchayat leaders, the Panchayat administration is streamlined and strengthened and innovative practices are developed while implementing the schemes and programmes.
- The best practices and the Panchayats involved in innovative practices have to be documented properly and scientifically and they have to be disseminated through the media.
- At present Panchayat institutions are not functioning as a system but in an individualistic way and in a leader centric or officer centric manner. Both officials and

leaders perceive Panchayat affairs are their affairs. Both the leaders and the officials as not well-versed in the rules of the game. To make the Panchayat as institution of self-government a series of appropriate steps have to be taken.

APPENDICES

APPENDIX-I

TRAINING SCHEDULE

Training for the Gram Panchayat Presidents on Panchayat Administration

	Time	Session	Title	Resource Persons
1st Day	9:30 to 10:30	I	Registration and Personal Counselling	Training Team
	10:30 to 11:30	II	Inauguration	VIP
	11:30 to 12:30	III	Principles of Decentralization, 73rd Constitutional Amendment Act	Dr. G. Palanithurai
	12:30 to 1:30	IV	Tamil Nadu Panchayat Act, 1994	Dr. G. Palanithurai
	1:30 to 2:30		Lunch Break	
	2:30 to 5:00	V	Gram Panchayat Administration Duties Responsibilities & Power Discussion, Q&A	Sri N.S. Chidambaram
	5:00 to 5:30	VI	Gram Sabha and People's Participation	Sri K. Vallinayagam
	5:30 to 6:00	VII	Review	Sri K. Vallinayagam

Contd.

Appendix-I (Contd.)

2nd Day	9:30 to 11:30	I	Multi-Level Planning in Gram Panchayat, Discussion	Sri N.S. Chidambaram
	11:30 to 1:00	II	Integration of Panchayat Plan and Sectoral Programmes and Discussion/Q&A	Sri K. Vallinayagam
	1:30 to 2:30		Lunch Break	
	2:30 to 4:30	III	Common Property Resource Management Protection of Natural Resources, Discussion/Q&A	Sri S. Krishnamoorthy
3rd Day	9:30 to 11:00	I	Financial Management Finance & Financial Resources, Discussion/Q&A	Sri S. Krishnamoorthy
	11:00 to 1:00	II	Maintenance of Accounts and Records and Audit Procedure, Discussion/Q&A	Sri K. Subramanian
	1:30 to 2:30		Lunch Break	
	2:30 to 4:00	III	Social Development & Social Justice, Discussion/Q&A	Dr. G. Palanithurai
	4:00 to 5:30	IV	Vision Building Exercise, Discussion/Q&A	Ms. G. Uma
	5:30 to 6:30	V	Leadership Building	Training Team

(Contd.)

Appendix-I (Contd.)

4th Day	9:30 to 11:00	I	Status of Indian Women/Rural Womenfolk - Social Citizenship - Society & Family related issues faced by women - Problem solving process - Gender equality role of individuals	Dr. A. Suriyakanthi
	11:00 to 1:00	II	Total Rural Sanitation	Dr. Regina Pappa
	1:00 to 2:00		Lunch Break	
	2:00 to 3:30	III	Social Development - Listing of Issues - Role of Women in Social Development - Role of Panchayat in Social Development	Mr. Ramani Mathew
	3:30 to 4:45	IV	Reproductive Child Health	IRH & F.W. Trust Staff
	4:45 to 6:00	V	Role of Panchayat in Economic Development	Dr. Palanithurai
	8:00		Dinner	

(Contd.)

Appendix-I (Contd.)

5th Day	9:00 to 1:00	I	Computer Orientation	Dr. Somasundaram
	1:00 to 2:00		Lunch Break	
	2:00 to 4:00	II	Exposure Visit to Gram Panchayat where computer is utilized	GRI Training Team
	4:30 to 5:00		Valedictory	

APPENDIX-II

PROFORMA – I

Capacity Building Exercise for Panchayat Presidents

1. Socio-Economic Profile of the Respondent

1.	Name:	
2.	Age:	
3.	Sex:	Male / Female
4.	Educational Qualification	
5.	Religion	
6.	Community	SC / BC / MBC / OC
7.	Occupation	Main Occupation: Sub-Occupation:
8.	Annual Income	
9.	Land-Holding	
10.	Family Status	Nuclear / Joint
11.	House details	(i) Own / Rented (ii) Tiled/hut/RCC/group house/unit
	(i) Electricity facility is available	Yes / No
	(ii) Toilet facility is available	Yes / No
	(iii) Drinking water tap connection	Yes / No
	(iv) Animal Husbandry is available	Yes / No
	If yes, specify total numbers of animals	
12.	Number of total family members	
13.	Party affiliation	Yes / No
	If yes, name of the party and position in the party	
14.	Details of association with social institutions	
15.	Which newspaper do you read	

APPENDIX-III

PROFROMA – II

2. Pre-Training Evaluation

1. Elected President for first time/second time?
2. Who encouraged you to contest in the election?
3. Reasons for your victory in the election?
4. After becoming President what are the leadership qualities acquired by you?
5. What are the basic features of the new Panchayat Raj System?
6. What are the characteristics of the 73rd Constitutional Amendment?
7. What are the duties and responsibilities of the Village Panchayat as per the Tamil Nadu Panchayat Act, 1994?
8. Explain the powers of the Gram Sabha.
9. How can people participate in the activities of the Gram Panchayat?
10. Give details of training you have undergone so far.
11. List the names of the Government programmes known to you?
12. What are your expectations from the training?

PROFORMA – III

3. Post-Training Evaluation

1. What are the objectives of the new Panchayat Raj System?
2. What do you mean by decentralization?
3. What are the implications of decentralization?
4. List the duties and responsibilities entrusted to the Gram Panchayat?
5. What are the duties and responsibilities entrusted to the President of the Gram Panchayat?
6. Explain the ways and means to augment financial resources.
7. What procedures have to be adhered to planning?
8. How are accounts to be maintained?
9. What are the activities to be undertaken for social development?
10. What are the leadership qualities needed by Panchayat Presidents?
11. How can economic development be achieved?
12. What are the activities to be carried out by the Panchayat administration for the development of *Dalits*?
13. What activities will result in the development of women?
14. What are your priorities in Panchayat administration?

APPENDIX-V

RESOURCE PERSONS

1. N.S. Chidambaram, Retd., Additional Director, Rural Development Department, Chennai.
2. K.Vallinayagam, Retd., Additional Director, Rural Development Department, Chennai.
3. S. Krishnamoorthy, Retd., Additional Director, Rural Development Department, Chennai.
4. K. Subramanian, Retd., Additional Director, Rural Development Department, Chennai.
5. Thiyagarajan, Retd., Additional Director, Rural Development Department, Chennai.
6. Dr. G. Palanithurai, Head, Department of Political Science and Development Administration, Gandhigram Rural Institute, Gandhigram, Dindigul.
7. Dr. V. Ragupathy, Reader, Department of Political Science and Development Administration, Gandhigram Rural Institute, Gandhigram, Dindigul.
8. Dr. A. Suriyakanthi, Director, Department of Adult Education, Gandhigram Rural Institute, Gandhigram, Dindigul.
9. Dr. K. Somasundaram, Head, Department of Computer Science & Application, Gandhigram Rural Institute, Gandhigram, Dindigul.
10. I. Kaspar Raj, System Programmer/System Analyst, Computer Centre, Gandhigram Rural Institute, Gandhigram, Dindigul.
11. Thangavel, Project Officer, GIRH & FW Trust, Ambathurai, Gandhigram, Dindigul.
12. Ramani Mathew, Lawyer, Dindigul.
13. Bimla Chandrasekar, Director, EKTA, Madurai.

14. M. Gurusamy, Research Assistant, Department of Political Science and Development Administration, Gandhigram Rural Institute, Gandhigram, Dindigul.
15. S. Devaraj, Research Assistant, Department of Political Science and Development Administration, Gandhigram Rural Institute, Gandhigram, Dindigul.
16. M.A. Thirunavukkarasu, Department of Political Science and Development Administration, Gandhigram Rural Institute, Gandhigram, Dindigul.
17. A. Thangathurai, Department of Political Science and Development Administration, Gandhigram Rural Institute, Gandhigram, Dindigul.
18. G. Uma, Department of Political Science and Development Administration, Gandhigram Rural Institute, Gandhigram, Dindigul.
19. K. Tamilarasan, Department of Political Science and Development Administration, Gandhigram Rural Institute, Gandhigram, Dindigul.
20. A. Geetha, Department of Political Science and Development Administration, Gandhigram Rural Institute, Gandhigram, Dindigul.

Bibliography

Bandhyopadhyay, D., Mukherjee, Amitava, Gavai, Mitali Sen, (2003) *Empowering Panchayats, Handbook for Master Trainers Using Participatory Approach*, New Delhi: Concept Publishing Company, (2003).

Palanithurai, G., (1997) "Capacity Building Exercise for Elected Representatives in Tamil Nadu", *Journal of Rural Development*, Vol.16, No.4 October-December.

Palanithurai, G., (1999) *A Report of the Training Programme conducted for Gram Panchayati Presidents and Vice-Presidents on Panchayati Raj Administration with special reference to Water Supply and Sanitation in Villupuram and Cuddalore Districts*, Gandhigram: Rajiv Gandhi Chair for Panchayati Raj Studies.

Palanithurai, G., (1999) *A Report of the Training Programme conducted for Gram Panchayat Presidents on Empowerment of Panchayati Raj Institutions on the issues of Population, Health and Social Development,* Gandhigram: Rajiv Gandhi Chair for Panchayati Raj Studies.

Palanithurai, G., (2000) *A Report of the Training Programme conducted for Gram Panchayati Women Presidents of Madurai, Ramanathapuram and Pudukkottai Districts,* Gandhigram: Rajiv Gandhi Chair for Panchayati Raj Studies, 2000.

Palanithurai, G., (2001) *Capacity Building for Local Body Leaders*, New Delhi: Concept Publishing Company.

Palanithurai, G., (2002) *A Report of the Capacity Building Programme for Panchayati Presidents of Dindigul District*, Gandhigram, Rajiv Gandhi Chair for Panchayati Raj Studies.

Palanithurai, G., (2002) *A Report of the Training Programme and Capacity Building Exercise conducted for Gram Panchayati Women Leaders of Pudukkottai District,* Gandhigram: Rajiv Gandhi Chair for Panchayati Raj Studies.

Palanithurai, G., (2002) *A Report of the Training Programme conducted for Gram Panchayat Presidents of Pudukkottai*

District, Gandhigram: Rajiv Gandhi Chair for Panchayati Raj Studies.

Palanithurai, G., (2002) *A Report of the Training Programme conducted for the Gram Panchayati Presidents on Total Rural Sanitation Programme*, Gandhigram: Rajiv Gandhi Chair for Panchayati Raj Studies, 2002.

Palanithurai, G., (2002) *A Report on Leadership Training and Capacity Building Exercise for Gram Panchayati women Leaders of Dindigul District*, Gandhigram: Rajiv Gandhi Chair for Panchayati Raj Studies, 2002.

Palanithurai, G., (2003) *A Report of the Capacity Building Programme for Gram Panchayati Presidents of Trichy District*, Gandhigram: Rajiv Gandhi Chair for Panchayati Raj Studies.

Palanithurai, G., (2003) *A Report of the Training Programme conducted for the Gram Panchayati Presidents on Total Rural Sanitation Programme*, Gandhigram: Rajiv Gandhi Chair for Panchayati Raj Studies.

Palanithurai, G., (2003) *A Report on Leadership Training and Capacity Building Exercise for Gram Panchayati Women Leaders of Trichy District*, Gandhigram: Rajiv Gandhi Chair for Panchayati Raj Studies.

Palanithurai, G., (2003) *New Panchayati Raj in Tamil Nadu (with the Act in Original)*, New Delhi: Concept Publishing Company.

Rajiv Gandhi Chair, (1997) *Manual for Capacity Building Exercises to the Local Body Exercises to the Local Body Leaders* (in Tamil), Gandhigram: Rajiv Gandhi Chair for Panchayati Raj Studies.

Rajiv Gandhi Chair, (2002) *Manual for Leadership Training for Women* (in Tamil), Gandhigram: Rajiv Gandhi Chair for Panchayati Raj Studies.

Index

Abolishing plastics and polythene, 123
Academic institutions, 2
Accountability, 7, 18
Accounting procedure, 27-28, 82-83, 107-08
Action Plan, 120
Age group, distribution of, 50
Achieving social justice, 18
Agencies or little republics, 132
Agitation, 146
Agricultural committee, 105
Agricultural cooperative society, 130
Agricultural waste, 149
AIADMK, 8
Alcohol preparation, 135
Allegations, 139-40
Annadurai, President of Maravamangalam Gram Panchayat, 130
Annual Tax Collection, 126
Anti-social activisim, 111
Anti-social elements, 46
Appipalayam Gram Panchayat, Karur district, 145
Approval of layouts, 26-27
Arumugam, President of Edaiyathimangalam Gram Panchayat, 134
Aslam, M., 3
Assessment of tax, 22
Auction-cum-tender procedure, 33
Auction notice, preparation of, 32-33
Audit formalities, 83
Audit report, procedure to be followed after the receipt of, 35
Authority to conduct auction of lease or sale, 32
Ayyar, S., 14, 128

Balwadis, 116, 133, 145
Bank Loans, 38
Basic amenities, 16, 82
Basic statistics, verification of, 36
Beevi, Jamruth, President of Devipattinam Gram Panchayat, 139
Behavioural Change (Women), inputs for, 45-46
Behaviour of the trainees, 47-48
Block Development Officer, training programmes, 111
Block Panchayat Leaders Federation, 137
Brahmadesam Gram Panchayat, 141
Briefing about the women federation, 46-47
Building civic culture, 18
Building leadership qualities, 44-45
Bureaucracy, 8, 131, 140
CAPART, Hyderabad, 13
Capacity building, 2-5
Central and State Government, programmes and schemes of, 4-5, 82-83, 97-98
Challenges, 140
Chidambaram, M. S., 45, 48
Child marriage, 109
Children's development, 110
Chinnamal, President of Urathupatti Gram Panchayat, 132
Choodamani, President of Karisalpatti Gram Panchayat, Dindigul district, 124
Collaboration with district administration, 13-14
Collective action by the community, 129-30
Collection of Taxes, 22

Common Property, 134
    encroachments of, 124
Common Property Resources, 105
    management, 144
Communal conflicts, 111
Community development, 139-40
Community distribution, 52
Community power, 124
Conscientization of the leaders, 43-44
Coonrod, John, 149
Controlling authorities, 30-31
Criticisms, 119
Dalits, 82-84, 141-42
    community, problems of, 142-43
    development, 95
    gram panchayat leaders, 116, 120, 140-44
        problems faced by, 140-42
    reservation for, 78
DANIDA, 123
Decentralization, 151
    concept of, 16-17
    impact of, 90
    implication of, 7
    objectives of, 17-18
    true spirit of, 12
Decentralization mean, 89-90
Decentralization Process, 19-20
Decentralization of Powers, 103
    objectives of, 6-7
Deepening democracy, 17
Demand driven participatory development, 19
Demand guidelines, 83
Democratic decentralization, 6, 11, 19-20
    new experiment of, 17
Departmental Management, 33
Deputy Block Development Officer, 14
    scrutiny of replies by, 35
Develop Leadership Qualities, 108
Development Institution, 2
Development issues, 120-21
Development Organizations, 152-53
Devipattinam Gram Panchayat, 139
Devolution of finance, 132
Devolution of Powers, 6-8, 119-20, 132-33
    process of, 20
Devolution in Tamil Nadu, 121
Dhanapakiam, President of Keelamavazangai Gram Panchayat, Villupur district, 127
Dindigul district, 13
Disbursement of funds, 102
Disputes, 77
District Panchayat Leaders Federation, 137
District Planning Committee, 38, 158
DMK, 8
Donation, 76
DRDA, 14
Drinking water crisis, 122, 127
Drinking water supply, 103, 157
Driking water management, 124
Drinking water sources, 145
Durairaj, President of Melachithalacheri Panchayat, 130

Economic development, 19, 129-30
    approaches to, 94-95
Edaiyathimangalam Gram Panchayat, 134
Education distribution, 51
Education Committee, 105
Effect of social development, 92-93
Elango, President of Koothampakkam Gram Panchayat, 129
Elavarasan, President of Shenbagarama Nallur Gram Panchayat, 142
Elected representative, roles and responsibilities of, 15
    training for, 16-17
Employment opportunities, 109, 131
Empowering women, 4, 7, 18
Ending child labour, 110
Environment and sanitation, 109

Environmental protection, 103, 145
Eswari, President of Appipalayam Gram Panchayat, Karur district, 145
Executive authority, functions of, 22-23

Family income and expenditure, collection of, 37, 57
Feedback from participation about training (Men), 112-13
Feedback from participation about the training (Women), 114-15
Field Visit, 49
Fighting against illegal mining, 146
Fighting against the mafia, 146
Financial constraints, 101
Financial sources, 91
Food security to the poor, 129-30
Ford Foundation, 3
Frustration, 18
Funds from NGOs, 38

Gandhi, Christudoss, 143
Gandhigram Gram Panchayat, 137
Gandhigram Rural Institute, 5, 11, 12, 46, 119, 137, 138, 144
Gandhigram Trust, 49
Gender sensitization, 43, 152
Globalization, 17
Good Government, 12
Gopala Krishnan, President of Brahmadesam Gram Panchayat, 141
Government programmes, 86
Government schemes, 3
Gram panchayat, audit disallowance and damage, 33
  agency functions of, 22
  capacity building exercises for, 13
  development plans, preparation of, 38
  discretionary functions of, 21
  duties and responsibilities of, 84, 90-92
  financial resources of, 106-07
  mandatory functions of, 21
  people participation in, 100
  roles and responsibilities of, 104-105
  sources of income of, 23-24
Gram Panchayat in IEC activities, 43
Gram Panchayat Leaders Federation, 137
Gram Panchayat Leaders, problems faced by, 121-22
Gram Panchayat Presidents, 16
  audit objections, 35
  dual role to be performed by, 83-84
  innovative practices, 45
  role and functions of, 99-100
  social development issues, 121
Gram Panchayat women leaders participation in the training programme, 96-97
Gram Sabha, 11
  activities, 84-85
  meeting expenditure for, 40-41
  plans of, 38-39
  operational ground to solve problem, 111
  resolutions of, 85
Grassroots movements, 6

Health Committee, 105
House Tax Collection, 126, 155
Human Rights Commission, 142
Hunger Project, 12, 46, 121, 132, 151

IEC activities, 42
Illango, Bhavani, President of Merapanai Khadu Gram Panchayat, 155
Illicit arrack mafia, 77
Illicit liquor brewers, 135
Illiteracy, 4
Implement Government Welfare Schemes, 109
Inauguration, 14-15
Information, 83
Infrastructure loans (HUDCO), 38
Initiatives and Innovations, 122-29

Interferences, 151-52
for development organizations, 152-53
for policy makers, 152

Japan, 15
Jayalalitha, Selvi J., 83

Kala, President of Moothulapuram Gram Panchayat, 142
Kakkanur Gram Panchayat, Villupuram district, 122
Kaliammal, President of Therkkupatti Gram Panchayat, 139
Karisalpatti Gram Panchayat, Dindigul district, 124
Keelamavazangai Gram Panchayat, Villipur district, 127
Koothampakkam Gram Panchayat, 44, 129
KVK, Gandhigram, 48

L. C. Jain Committee, 9
Landholdings, distribution of, 54
Leadership, learning process, 16
qualities of, 44, 83, 93-94
Lease deed, 33
Leases by panchayats, 31-32
Licence fees, levy of, 24
Linkage between media and grassroots governance, 147-48
Local self-Government, 13

Maintenance of accounts, procedure, 92-93
Managing Panchayats, 144-47
Maravamangalam Gram Panchayat, 130
Marudambal, President of Panchampatti Gram Panchayat, 138
Media and Governance, 147-48
Melachithalacheri Gram Panchayat, 130
Meeting procedure, 27-28
Merpanaikkadu Gram Panchayat, 135
Methodology, 49-50
Micro-level planning, 16, 152
Minor minerals revenue, 156
MLA/MPs factors, 83
solve the problems of the people, 83

Nallukkottai Gram Panchayat, 129
Narayanasamy, S., 151
Natham Poramboke, 76, 79
National Institute of Rural Development, 2
New Panchayati Raj System, 9, 16, 102, 155
basic structure of, 98-99
objectives of, 89-90
perception of, 84
Non-conventional Energy Sources, 122
Non-Governmental Development organizations, 3, 7
Noor Mohammad, President of Sarkaraikottai Gram Panchayat, Ramnad district, 131
Noothulapuram Gram Panchayat, 142
Nutritious noon meal scheme, 132

Observations, 149-50, 154-60
Occupations, distribution of, 53
Odanthurai Gram Panchayat, Coimbatore district, 126
Open house discussion, 148-49
Operational ground to solve problem, 111

Palanithurai, G., 15, 17, 44, 48, 121, 148
Palanithurai, K.V., 136
Palanisamy, V., 150
Panchampatti Gram Panchayat, 138
Panchayati Raj Institutions (PRIs), 16
constraints and handicaps in, 16
financial position in, 102
Panchayats,
common properties of, 28-29
development activities, 85
functionaries, 8

roles and functions, 2
strategies to enhance the economic position of, 108-09
trials and triumphs of, 119-53
Panchayat activities, priorities of, 110
Panchayat administration, 10, 13, 21, 151
activities of, 105-08
problems of, 14
rules and procedures of, 11
Panchayat finance, 23-24
Panchayat management, innovations in, 155
Panchayat plans, 132
Panchayat transparent activities, 124
Panchayati Raj System, 3, 9, 15, 82, 119, 154-55
objectives of, 102
Panchayat leaders, 12
power and responsibilities, 119-20
problems faced, 72-73
problems and obstacles faced, 120
roles and responsibilities, 9, 28-29
Panchayat Presidents, capacity building exercise for, 166
embarrassing situation, 101
functions and responsibilities, 104
misappropriated funds, 10
problems of, 10-12
proper maintenance of accounts, 107-08
schemes and programmes, 160-61
socio-economic profile, 166
Peace Committee, 105
Perambur Gram Panchayat, 136
Participatory rural appraisal, method of, 37-38
Planning Committee, 105
formation of, 36
Planning process, steps of, 107
Planning procedures, 91-92
Plastic free villages, 122
Poramboke, 29, 156
Possessing of electricity facility, distribution of, 55
Possessing of toilet facility, 56
Post-training evaluation (men), 88-96
Post-training evaluation (women), 96-101, 102-111
Post-training evaluation, 168
Pre-training evaluation (men), 82-87, 167
Primary health centre, 116
Professional tax, 75
Protection to the Presidents, 30
Pucca water management system, 124
Public contributions, 38
Public distribution system, 129
Pudukkottai, 13
Puvaloor Gram Panchayat, 134

Raghavan, B.S., 140
Ragupathy, V., 122, 146
Rain water harvesting, 110, 116, 122, 125
Rajiv Gandhi Chair, 3, 4, 12
help the training programme, 13-14
Ramanathapuram, 13
Ration cards, 133
Re-auction, 33
Reduce corruption, 116
Regional Extension Training Centres, 2
Religion distribution, 52
Remove bogus ration cards, 77
Reservation for SC/ST people, 98
Reservation for women and *dalits*, 98-99, 123, 154
Resolutions, 116
Resource mobilization, 16
Revenue from forestry, 159
Rural development department, schemes implemented, 86
Rural development schemes, 100
Rural housing, 129-30
Rural sanitation programme funds, 41-42
Safe drinking water, 133
Sampath, C., 121
Sanitation programme, 126
implementation procedure of, 41-43

Sarin, Rita, 150
Sarakaraikottai Gram Panchayat, Ramnad district, 131
Saving promotion, 110
Security deposit, 32
Self-Helf Group (SHGs), 104, 105, 129, 135, 145
Shenbagarama Nallur Gram Panchayat, 142
Siruthondanallor Gram Panchayat, Ramanathapuram, 144
Singapore, 15
Sivangangai, 13
Social development, 41-42
Socio-economic background (men), 50-60
Socio-economic background (women), 61-71
Solid waste management, 129, 139
South Korea, 15
State Election Commission, 99, 150
State and Central Governments, schemes of, 101-02
Statutory grants - receipts, 24
Swajaldhara scheme, 79
Swaminathan Committee, 159
64th Constitutional Amendment Bill, 8, 19
73rd Constitutional Amendment Act, 1, 8, 18, 20
basic principles of, 88-89

Taiwan, 15
Tamil Nadu, experience of decentralization in, 6-12
Tamil Nadu Panchayat Act, 4, 10, 22, 82, 99
Taxes, 24-26
advertisement tax, 25
house tax, 24
professional tax, 25
tax on agricultural land, 26
Therkkupatti Gram Panchayat, 139
Thiruvasi Gram Panchayat, 146
Three-tier Panchayat System, 8, 98
Thuvarankurichi Town Panchayat, 137
Tiruchirappalli, 13
Total rural sanitation programme, 124
Trainees, consultation of, 47
expectation, 46
issues of, 47
questions raised by, 74-75, 78-82
Training, areas, 87-88
manual, 3
methodology, 4
nature of, 48-49
policy, 2
programmes, 3-5, 11-12, 85-88
utility of, 102
Training Institutions, 2
Training for Gram Panchayat President on Panchayat Administration, 162-65
TWAD Board drinking water supply scheme, 125
Type of family, distribution of, 54-55

Udayamoorthy, M. S., 128
Uma (coordinator for training the women), 45
United funds, 152
Upgrading of local skills, 19
Urathupatti Gram Panchayat, 132

Valedictory function, 149
Veedu Panchayat, 118
Vellimalaipattinam Gram Panchayat, 145
Venkatasubramanian, A.K., 131
Vepankulam Gram Panchayat, Sivagangai district, 133
Vigilance Committee, 105
Village Panchayats, 159-60

Water management and sanitation, 122
Women and child welfare and health facilities, 103
Women and *dalit*, issues of, 137
development plan, 159
Women development, 95, 110

Women empowerment, 109-10
Women's participation, 98
Women Panchayat leaders, 140, 151
 annual income, 66
 responses of, 103-05
 roles and responsibilities, 103-05
Women Panchayat President, basic features of, 99-100
 community, distribution of, 63
 educational qualification, 62
 house owned, 67
 household facilities of, 69
 landholdings, 65
 occupation, 64
 political party affiliation, 70
 responses of, 102
 training programmes, 101-02, 110-12
 types of family, 67-68
 vision of, 116-18
Women representatives, experience of, 136-38
 valedictory programme, 47

Youth club, 104

Zamindars, 154